BENEATH THE VEIL
Fall of the House of Saud

David Oualaalou

authorHOUSE®

AuthorHouse™
1663 Liberty Drive
Bloomington, IN 47403
www.authorhouse.com
Phone: 1 (800) 839-8640

Published by AuthorHouse 10/27/2018

ISBN: 978-1-5462-5852-0 (sc)
ISBN: 978-1-5462-5850-6 (hc)
ISBN: 978-1-5462-5851-3 (e)

Library of Congress Control Number: 2018910795

Print information available on the last page.

Cover Design and Photograph of the Author by Elizabeth Ann

Contents

Acknowledgments

In honor of those who, despite overwhelming odds, remain dedicated to their cause and speak truth to power…

Preface

Just for a moment consider the following scenario in the kingdom of Saudi Arabia: a plot to assassinate the new king; a twist into a saga of a monarchy in chaos, the revelations of dark secrets, the love of money, the drama, the corruption, and the royal characters. The outcome could be a blockbuster movie of the year. Few years ago, this storyline would have been dismissed as too far-fetched. But today it is not fiction. Rather it is reality through which darks secrets are emerging. Disappearance of princes in the night intensifies. Rendition flights intrigue, detention and torture of royal members, including one of the world's richest men, in the luxurious Ritz-Carlton hotel persist, deals with loyalists behind closed doors persevere, and corruption at the highest level runs amok. The emergence of these dark secrets reveals a sinister reality, that of a kingdom in a downward spiral. A reality that demands the attention of diplomats, global affairs analysts, intelligence officers, investors, the Chinese, the Russians, the Muslim world, and those with a panache for the lavish lifestyle of Middle Eastern royalties.

Nearing his death, a venerable king, Salman bin Abdulaziz Al Saud, names one of his sons, Mohammed bin Salman (MbS), as heir to the kingdom. The young son prematurely takes the reins of power. Naïve about international affairs, he immediately falls into various ill-conceived foreign-policy intrigues, including supporting armed factions in rival countries. The crown prince fears for his future at home, too, so he silences activists and would-be rivals within his country. Only months later, witnesses near the palace report the sound of gunshots, and observers speak openly of an assassination attempt on the crown prince. International reports speculate that he is dead; his subsequent "appearances" are shrouded in secrecy.

The idea of writing *Beneath the Veil: Fall of the House of Saud* became pressing to me after completing my second book, *Volatile State: Iran in the Nuclear Age*. While researching for new perspectives and untested theories, I came across a plethora of sources on the future of the Middle East's geopolitical landscape in the aftermath of the current civil war in Syria. The devastation and instability in Iraq, the expansion of Islamic State in Iraq and Syria (ISIS) throughout the Middle East and North Africa (MENA) region and beyond, Turkey's and Iran's flexing their military and political muscles, and the escalating tensions between Saudi Arabia and Iran are examples. Analysis points to Saudi Arabia as one of two key regional players—the second is Iran—in the unfolding drama of the Middle East.

Before continuing, I will offer my qualifications to the reader, specifically, my preparation for assessing the geopolitics of the Kingdom of Saudi Arabia. For more than ten years, I worked with elite US military forces carrying out operations by order of US policymakers. I visited Saudi Arabia, lived there, and worked there, officially representing the United States government, on many occasions. I speak Arabic fluently, grasp the depth of the kingdom's social, cultural, and religious interactions, and, from both abstract and practical perspectives, know how Saudi Arabia's internal politics work. This firsthand experience is necessary, in my opinion, to offer the most salient analysis of how the desert kingdom interacts, responds, and manages its role within the current geopolitical landscape of the Middle East and the Muslim world writ large. Regarding my personal experience, please bear in mind that, though this work discusses unclassified and declassified information, it does not, and *cannot*, offer evidence from classified sources.

That said, I draw on those experiences to help both individual readers and broader audiences understand the political realities of the Middle East. I seek to share insights on how to solve the problems affecting both the Middle East and the world. My frequent writings have already contributed to understanding these important concerns. I have authored op-ed. pieces on global affairs for the Slovak Atlantic Council, an affiliate of the European Atlantic Council; the *HuffPost*; the *Waco Tribune-Herald*; *South China Morning Post* (Hong Kong), and the World Affairs Council (Austin, Texas). My articles have been translated into Arabic, Chinese,

Farsi, French, German, Malay, Russian, Thai, Turkish, and Spanish, among other languages. Those articles address a wide range of topics that include global energy markets, international security, global affairs, US foreign policy, international business, and more. Occasionally, I describe how the geopolitical landscape in the Middle East may look in the next decade or so and how certain countries, including Saudi Arabia, may act or react given the seismic shifts shaping the political landscape, regionally and globally. I am also the author of two books, *The Ambiguous Foreign Policy of the United States: More than a Handshake* (2016) and *Volatile State: Iran in the Nuclear Age* (2018).

Like the previous two books, this book is not an editorial; it informs not only people who keep up with current events but also students of foreign policy, specifically, those considering a career in international affairs. It also informs industry leaders, helping them both to understand the impact of global politics on markets and economic trends and to make sense of the complex mix of geopolitical risks and economic opportunities. My analysis also draws from the writings of top scholars on the history, culture, and politics of Saudi Arabia and, more broadly, of international relations, and from leading scholarship on the Middle East. The research here is from academic journals, books, and other scholarly writings. It should appeal therefore to academics, foreign-policy professionals, international affairs analysts, policymakers, and the military establishment. This book also benefits business leaders in the energy sector, financial institutions, business associations, and investors. It provides them with analysis of geopolitical trends and the political, economic, and security risks that organizations face when working in the region. From a business perspective, my insights are key to an organization's long-term strategic planning and access to new markets not only in Saudi Arabia, but also in the Middle East.

I want the international business community in particular to question the assumption that "Saudi Arabia's oil will continue to give it a powerful voice in the international community." Conventional wisdom suggests that, given its oil wealth, Saudi Arabia always will be in a position to (a) influence regional politics and (b) impact global oil market prices. That assumption held true in the 1980s and 1990s. However, subsequent regional political and economic realities suggest otherwise. Given all the chaos in the region and Saudi Arabia's role in fomenting that chaos, one must see that Saudi Arabia's role will become even blurrier and more irrelevant. Even Saudi Arabia realizes that it lacks the political influence to affect events in the Middle East as they occur.

My interest in writing about Saudi Arabia focuses on both its *political influence* and its *economic role* in the Middle East. On the first point, one must analyze Saudi Arabia's political conflicts with neighboring countries. Clearly, Saudi Arabia aims to influence the political outcome in the region to its favor. Yet, the kingdom is lost in a maelstrom of conflicts as it reacts to one problem after another. The kingdom's reactions destabilize the region. For example, Saudi Arabia's ongoing ground and air strikes in Yemen have failed to achieve their objectives. These impulsive responses, if they continue, will affect Saudi Arabia more than any other country in the Middle East. The second reason for writing on Saudi Arabia is economic, specifically, the kingdom's role in influencing oil prices. Unlike Turkey, Egypt, Iraq, and Syria, nations impacted by the region's ongoing titanic geopolitical shifts, Saudi Arabia is more likely to feel that impact given its oil richness, religious outreach, and political influence in the Muslim world. After publishing *Volatile State: Iran in the Nuclear Age*, I find it paramount to show why Saudi Arabia stands to face far greater difficulties in the Middle East than any other country precisely because of its political and economic influence.

Often, political uncertainties in the Middle East affect economic realities. The region's recent, sustained geopolitical shift brings with it a new geopolitical *outlook*, which compels Saudi Arabia to make difficult decisions about how to respond. Saudi Arabia must think about both how to keep its limited leadership role from declining further and how to develop new sources of revenue as oil prices continue to drop. Consider, for example, that Russia, a non- Organization of the Petroleum Exporting Countries (OPEC) member, recently agreed with Saudi Arabia, an OPEC member, to cut oil production in the hope of (a) countering the ongoing decrease in oil prices, and (b) harming Iran economically. Saudi Arabia could flatter itself into thinking that Russia favors the desert kingdom over Iran. However, such a reading overlooks Russia's increased cooperation with Iran. Further, Saudi Arabia should be concerned as Iran rejoins the international community through economic ventures with Russia and several countries from Asia, Europe, and other parts of the world. In bygone days, Saudi Arabia fancied itself Russia's favorite. But today, Russia is playing both sides by entering into an agreement with the Kingdom of Saudi Arabia (KSA) on oil production, on the one hand, and signing military and energy contracts with Iran, on the other. Careful observers see that Iran is raising its international profile with the indirect support of Russia and China while Turkey gains political influence in the region.

Meanwhile, the United States' role has become more limited and regressive. These developments will affect the political and economic future of the desert kingdom, specifically, whether the international community can still perceive Saudi Arabia as a regional leader given Iran's growing political, economic, military, and ideological expansion in the Middle East. For its part, Iran is uncertain what to make of Saudi Arabia's ongoing failed military engagement in Yemen, its support of Sunni rebels in Syria, and the latest conflict with Qatar. Saudi Arabia accuses Qatar of supporting terrorist groups, an accusation criticized by Iran. Iran's criticism comes on the heels of President Trump's recent trip to Saudi Arabia, which set the stage for the desert kingdom's aggressive behavior. Iran argues that the trip provided Saudi Arabia, along with its allies in the conflict [United Arab Emirates (UAE), Egypt, and Bahrain], with unrestricted power to act at its own discretion, in spite of international law, legal norms, and cultural traditions. Will it benefit Saudi Arabia that the United States could provide it [KSA] further opportunities to provide clandestine financial and logistical support to Sunni groups with a penchant for radical views and violent activities in the region and beyond?

The ongoing rhetoric in Washington over Iran has led to the question whether the United States is ready to engage Iran militarily on Saudi Arabia's behalf. Most analyses point in that direction, a dangerous path, to say the least! President Trump withdrew the United States from participation in Iran's 2015 nuclear agreement with the West. Is the United States now willing to embark on yet another disastrous policy in the Middle East, this time under President Trump? Is the United States entertaining the prospect of regime change in Iran? I hope not. Pursuing regime change in Iran will inevitably unleash unrelenting battles between the Shia (Iran) and Sunni (Saudi Arabia) variants of Islam. Mr. Trump's mere *consideration* of such a policy suggests that he lacks—and needs to acquire—the necessary political, social, religious, and cultural knowledge associated with the ever-changing dynamics of the Middle East. Alarmingly, President Trump has set his sights on Iran as Congress approves a new round of sanctions after US withdrawal from the agreement. Once again, is President Trump ready to engage Iran militarily on Saudi Arabia's behalf?

For *its* part, the Iranian regime is excited about *its own* engagement with the world, despite some limitations, after its nuclear agreement with the West. These developments raise concerns not only within *the Saudi monarchy* about its own survival, but also within *the international community* regarding the monarchy's stability. Saudi Arabia has slashed clumsily at Iran's economy through deep cuts in oil output in response to a drop in oil prices. Disturbingly, the Saudi royal family's internal power struggles have spilled over into the international press following the advancement of Prince Mohammed Bin Salman (MbS) to next in line for the Saudi throne. As revelations of arrests and interrogations of deposed heirs fill the pages of *The Wall Street Journal*, the Saudis can no longer keep their internal squabbles secret. Now laid bare, those familial power struggles have worsened tensions within the kingdom and have exacerbated anxieties throughout the international community over the kingdom's present and future stability.

Moreover, Saudi Arabia has to ponder whether it can counter Iran's growing influence in the Middle East. Consider, for example, the opportunity that Iran saw in Iraq after the US invasion of 2003, an opportunity that came to fruition once US forces withdrew from Iraq. Iran's influence in Iraq now encompasses all aspects of Iraqi society, ranging from military and political affairs to social and religious matters. Saudi Arabia must answer that question in view of Iran's recent nuclear agreement with the West, an agreement that all but makes Iran a nuclear power, regardless of the US's withdrawal from the agreement. Can Saudi Arabia respond to the social demands of its young population given the high unemployment rate? Will it pivot, finally, toward Asia, mainly China, for economic stability as the United States disengages from the Middle East after its own failed policies there, including its support of torture in Yemen? I am convinced that Saudi Arabia—whose survival, for much of its existence as a nation, has depended on the United States—may soon face an existential crisis since Iran, its archenemy, is well positioned, politically speaking, to outmaneuver the Saudis and thereby gain the voice of leadership within the region. How will Saudi Arabia deal with such a crisis if it cannot depend on the US? There is an increased urgency to answering these questions. Saudi Arabia recognizes that its nemesis Iran, now more than ever, is closer to achieving its political objective: to become a regional power with the prestige and influence to orchestrate the region's political course and leave Saudi Arabia by the wayside. Two facts add urgency to the situation. First, Tehran and Riyadh ceased diplomatic relations, in January 2016. Second, Iran abhors the Saudi royal family, a claim supported by Ali Noorani's June 23, 2017, article "Chants against Saudi Royals as Iran Marks Jerusalem Day." Such animosity highlights the intensifying battle of will over influence and dominance in the Middle East between the two rivals.

Against this backdrop, I argue that the Kingdom of Saudi Arabia's foreign and domestic policies under the leadership of its ailing monarch, King Salman, have to adapt to the new exigencies. Simultaneously, I wonder what will become of Saudi Arabia when King Salman—eighty-three years old at the time of this writing—passes away, when his impulsive, inexperienced son, Crown Prince Mohammed Bin Salman, ascends to the throne.

Global-affairs analysts and Saudi watchers have voiced concern that the death of the Saudi king will set off power struggles within the royal family. Will the rest of the royal family accept Crown Prince Mohammed Bin Salman and allow him to rule, or, to the contrary, will the kingdom's royal family still see division within its ranks after the current king's demise? Saudi Arabia went through similar internal turmoil, in 1975, when King Faisal Bin Abdulaziz Al Saud was assassinated. Given the present familial tumult and the inevitable shift in the Middle East's political landscape, the risk to the desert kingdom's stability is the greatest that it has been since the assassination of King Faisal, in 1975. I predict that Saudi Arabia's governing house will be shaken to its foundations, if and when Crown Prince Mohammed Bin Salman ascends to the throne. Worse yet, the political and social turmoil inside the kingdom will inevitably spill across the greater, strife-torn Middle East. Is it possible that such instability could set Saudi Arabia and Iran on a collision course to battle, as Iran and Iraq did in the 1980s?

This book, then, is specifically about whether Saudi Arabia can maintain its leadership in the Middle East or the Muslim world, for that matter. That question depends, to a large extent, on its religious identity. Saudi Arabia is the birthplace of Islam. Two of Islam's holiest sites—Mecca and Madinah—are located in Saudi Arabia. This historical good fortune offers the kingdom a simulacrum of religious authority, which it uses, conveniently, to pursue its political agenda, one veiled in a religious narrative. Saudi Arabia takes it upon itself to dictate to the Muslim world how to worship, conduct itself, and manage its religious affairs, but why? This question deserves an answer. Yet, some scholars, mainly in the Muslim world, out of ignorance or from fear of retaliation, refrain from answering the question. And yet, the question *needs* to be answered so that the Muslim world can recalculate the *exact* value of Saudi religious authority. That religious authority, after all, *is* the currency in which Saudi Arabia trades in the marketplace of ideas. To question the value of that currency is to question the value of Wahhabism. It is to question the truth of the teachings—more succinctly, the ideology—of Sheikh Mohammed Ibn Abdul Wahhab, a prominent eighteenth-century Hanbali Muslim cleric, who followed the most conservative school of jurisprudence in Sunni Islam. I address Wahhabism in this book in great detail. Suffice it to say for now that the Wahhabist interpretations of Islam are like twisted fingers that reach into the dark corners of the Middle East, extending even into Afghanistan, Pakistan, and Africa. Wahhabism is the hand that misguides many of the ventures undertaken by Saudi Arabia in the Middle East and abroad. One cannot forget religion when reflecting on Saudi Arabia's short- and long-term strategies. The Saudis themselves are preoccupied with Iran's growing capabilities and how its increasing power strengthens its *religious* influence, at least within the regions festering with the ongoing conflict between Sunni (primarily in Saudi Arabia) and Shiite (dominant in Iran).

Indeed, Saudi Arabia's historical religious identity plays out every day in contemporary politics. Saudi Arabia's religious identity has been under the microscope since the attacks of 9/11 on New York and the Pentagon, and Saudi Arabia's connections to some of the terrorists involved in the plot, including Osama bin Laden. Further, the desert kingdom faces scrutiny in the light of WikiLeaks' recent disclosure of an email in which former presidential candidate Hillary Clinton shared information suggesting that Saudi Arabia has been funding both ISIS and radical Sunni groups. The disclosure clearly indicates the Wahhabist ideology at work.

This work focuses on two important questions: 1) Will Saudi Arabia weather the geopolitical storm that rages across the Middle East? As the storm intensifies, a desire for survival should compel Saudi Arabia to rethink the safety of the shelter that its traditional alliance with the United States has provided. US leadership continues to recede in the Middle East as Russia and China increase their presence in the region. Consider, for example, Russia's intention of building a permanent base in Syria in addition to its already extant Soviet-era naval base in Tartus. Russia's presence highlights its long-term strategy, in which it seeks to influence the changing balance of power in the Middle East. Interestingly, Russia recently has stated that it considers Iran a strategic partner. I argue that this strategic rapprochement will change political calculations for everyone, mainly Saudi Arabia. How the Kingdom of Saudi Arabia intends to engage other major powers, mainly Russia and China, greatly interests this work; 2) Can Saudi Arabia keep its people happy as the kingdom loses oil revenue? Given the ongoing decline in oil prices, Saudi Arabia has been forced to dip into its financial reserves—about $655 billion, by some estimates—to support the royal family's lavish lifestyle while unemployment among the Saudi youth balloons, and young people feel more and more discontented.

As the Middle East descends into greater chaos, Saudi Arabia will find it harder to maintain its equilibrium if it lacks a strategy to contend with force-producing events. The United States also must reconsider its relations with, and support for, Saudi Arabia while evaluating how the US should adjust its policy toward both the kingdom and the greater region. The urgency for the US is clear. It must avoid being pulled into the centuries-old ideological spat between Iran and Saudi Arabia. Yet, one cannot assume that the US-Saudi relationship will stay constant and stable when both Saudi Arabia and the United States' strategic interests are at stake. Never before in their history have the two allies faced such a predicament, one that may force them to go their separate ways in search of a solution.

And so, the stage is set. Iran gains power, through alliances with Russia and China, as the United States, Saudi Arabia's long-time superpower ally, looks far less than super in the Middle East. The wealth and power of the Saudi royal family declines as oil prices drop. Consequently, the Saudi royal family fights within itself as the venerable Saudi monarch's day of death draws near. All the while, Saudi Arabia undertakes shortsighted, costly ventures in the Middle East; a twisted religious ideology lies at the heart of its misadventures. I write this book with the absolute conviction that Saudi Arabia has been using its oil wealth and its interpretation of the Wahhabist ideology to gain an advantage. Will the desert kingdom be able to continue as it has, or must it change its course given the shifting sands of the Middle East? *Beneath the Veil: Fall of the House of Saud* addresses these and other relevant questions.

CHAPTER I

Introduction: An Overview

The Kingdom of Saudi Arabia (KSA) is playing catch-up. As it hurriedly deals with one issue, another leaps forward, forcing the desert kingdom into a vicious circle of conflicts. All the while, it mistakes a mirage of its past leadership role for reality, but that leadership role has long since ceased to exist. This chapter addresses six themes to provide business, intelligence, foreign affairs, and academic communities both a clearer picture and an in-depth understanding of this controversial, intriguing, complicated, and ultraconservative Muslim monarchy.

This chapter offers a brief account of the political climate in the Middle East with Saudi Arabia as its focus. It includes topics such as Saudi-Chinese relations and what those mean for the political and economic future of the Middle East; the impact, if any, that renewed cooperation between Russia and Saudi Arabia may have in the region; and US-Saudi relations given the regional upheavals and resulting geopolitical shifts. To what degree and with what consequences will the Saudi royal family's internal struggle over succession further destabilize the monarchy? Will Saudi Arabia's Wahhabist ideology finally fall in upon its adherents, leading to the kingdom's own collapse? These issues are addressed with new insights, expanded knowledge, and answers to questions avoided for far too long.

As desert sands pass through the hourglass of history, Saudi Arabia realizes that its impulsive strategies and ill-conceived policies no longer serve its interests. Whoever would have thought that, in this era of chest pounding, the desert kingdom would finally reach out to Iraq to mend relations between Riyadh and Tehran? Yet, this Saudi initiative

1

stemmed not only from the complexities of the Middle East current political landscape, but also the realization from within the kingdom of its declining clout.[1] Now that Iran has reached an agreement with the West over its nuclear program, how will that outcome affect Saudi Arabia politically, economically, and socially? Consider what will become of the desert kingdom given the Middle East's geopolitical shifting. Consider furthermore the impact of lower oil prices on the already sluggish Saudi economy.

More than the preceding concerns, regional conflicts in the Middle East dominate and dictate the course of action the Saudi leadership must address. For example, the civil war in Syria shows no signs of abating. Anarchy in Yemen exacerbates tension between Iran and Saudi Arabia. Ongoing sectarian violence in Iraq fuels conflict between Shiites and Sunnis across the region. Political and security instability in Egypt is tentative. The failed state of Libya has opened the door for Russian support of self-appointed militias. Moreover, the kingdom's regional allies Egypt, United Arab Emirates (UAE), and Bahrain assist the ongoing Saudi Arabian blockade against Qatar.

The balance of power in the Middle East has shifted. Saudi Arabia realizes how challenging it has become to influence events on the ground given Iran's growing influence, absent US leadership, Russia and China's increasing footprints as they reshape the region's political and economic outcomes to their favor, and Europe's undertaking major economic ventures with Iran. Add to those the power dynamics within the Saudi royal family given the elevation of prince Mohammed Bin Salman (MbS) to crown prince, next in line to the throne.

Behind the scenes, business leaders, global-affairs analysts, and security analysts now debate MbS's competence to lead the Kingdom of Saudi Arabia after he receives full power from his ailing father, King Salman. Acting presumably in Saudi Arabia's interest, MbS impulsively conducted ground and air strikes on rebel-held areas in Yemen. That ill-conceived military action—which failed to defeat the Houthi rebels—raises serious humanitarian concerns. Saudi ground and air strikes have been partly responsible for displacing more than three million Yemenis and spreading famine.[2]

One common theme surfaces during debates and discussions about Saudi Arabia. The common theme: once perceived as a global player—primarily due to its oil wealth—Saudi Arabia's political influence and economic impact in the Middle East and beyond are waning. Unlike the state of affairs 20 or 30 years ago, current geopolitical dynamics in the Middle East have changed the conversation regarding the KSA's ability to manage such force-producing events. Now with many more players, new and old, the Middle East brings with it a new political order, different thinking, and the need for a new strategy. This new outcome is forcing Saudi Arabia to be reactive rather than proactive. The desert kingdom has never been in similar situations because it never has had to deal with, or even be concerned about, Iran's increasing influence, China and Russia's growing presence in the region, Turkey's aggressive foreign policy in the region, and the ongoing chaos in neighboring Yemen and Syria. The KSA has yet to figure out its strategy to deal with such threatening upheavals.

Global-affairs analysts, business leaders, and security analysts today are asking many serious questions. Particularly, what role, if any, does Saudi Arabia contemplate for itself in the new order of the Middle East? Although Saudi Arabia knows that it is in its best interest, politically and economically, to reconsider its policy toward Iran, will it do so? Will Saudi Arabia retain its religious leadership in the Muslim world now that the world scrutinizes its Wahhabist ideology? Saudi Arabia looks politically vulnerable given the multitude of problems in the Middle East today.

Saudi Arabia must also address its economic outlook following the drop in oil prices on the global market. The KSA's concern about the region's economic outcome depends largely on what Iran can achieve economically. As it stands, Iran rejoins the international community through economic ventures with Russia, China, France, India, Germany, Denmark, and Austria, among others. Simultaneously, Saudi Arabia's domestic tensions include high unemployment, continuing restrictions against Saudi women, and discrimination against its Shi'a minority. The KSA's ongoing relegation to second-class subjects of Shi'a in the eastern province creates ill will. Add to that a rebellion of unemployed, disgruntled Saudi youth in Riyadh, Jeddah, Dammam, or Qatif, and one may wake up to a country in chaos.[3]

Undoubtedly, Saudi Arabia's latest gesture to Iran, through Iraq, to restore diplomatic ties stems not from the KSA's desire to strengthen the ties of Islamic brotherhood. Rather, it stems from the KSA's fear of being left out in the cold once Iran holds the keys to the economic and political engine of the greater Middle East. It would be naïve to think that Iran could achieve this objective by itself. This effort will be well coordinated with Russia and China since doing so provides all three players a strategic incentive to continue working together despite different agendas and separate long-term goals. Nevertheless, for the KSA's sake, it makes sense to think strategically to ensure its positive involvement in the region's affairs regardless of their complexity. Toward that end, Saudi Arabia must evacuate and rebuild Yemen, reinstate diplomatic ties—if only on a limited basis—with its archenemy Iran, and diversify its economy from oil.

Equally important, a diplomatic initiative toward Iran could prove to be a shrewd tactic for the KSA. Specifically, Saudi Arabia could lessen fear within the Muslim world by talking with Iran. Talks would allow the KSA to hold onto its status as the leader—in words but not in deeds. By contrast, to argue that Iran's growing influence represents a threat to the entire Sunni Muslim world is nonsense; Crown Prince MbS's argument suggesting that Iran is going to take over the Muslim world is baseless. Those who are familiar with the history of tensions between Sunnis and Shiite since the death of Prophet Mohamed in 632 AD observe that the two branches of the faith will not see eye to eye, and I predict that that will not change anytime soon.[4] Interestingly, Saudi Arabia and Iran have cooperated in the past, mainly in the 1960s, and joined forces to address challenges and threats to both countries. Alexei Vassiliev writes, "In the mid-1960s, Saudi Arabia and Iran grew closer. Both countries were monarchies with an interest in suppressing revolutionary movements in the Middle East as a whole, and in the Gulf in particular. They also had a common interest in confronting Egypt, which was then the leader of the anti-royalist and anti-Western camp in the region."[5] Given the ongoing dynamics, and based on Iran's strategic thinking, I believe Iran's aspirations are hegemonic in nature: economically based, politically driven, and ideologically motivated.[6]

The present work devotes a chapter to addressing the religious question and the KSA's relationship to the Wahhabist ideology. The kingdom's religious identity has been under the microscope following the attacks of 9/11 on New York City and the Pentagon. The question centers on the nature and extent of Saudi Arabia's connections to some of the terrorists involved in the plot, including Osama bin Laden. Similarly, the KSA faces scrutiny given WikiLeaks' recent disclosure suggesting that Saudi Arabia has been funding both ISIS and radical Sunni groups. The disclosure clearly indicates the Wahhabist ideology at work.

On the opposite end of the spectrum, Iran raises its international profile with the indirect support of Russia and China following its nuclear agreement with the West. This comes on the heels of the United States' limited leadership, ambiguous foreign policy, and absence of a clear strategy for the Middle East. Will it benefit Saudi Arabia that the United States' limited role gives the KSA more opportunities to provide clandestine financial and logistic support to Sunni groups with a penchant for radical views and violent activities in the region and beyond? Possibly, but not conclusively!

Current developments in the Middle East affect the political and economic future of the desert kingdom. Will Saudi Arabia still be perceived as a regional leader after Iran's growing political, economic, military, and ideological expansion in the region? While Iran somehow is pleased with the ongoing upheavals in Yemen that further deepen Saudi Arabia's involvement, Tehran is uncertain what to make of Saudi Arabia's ongoing failed military engagement in Yemen, its support of Sunni rebels in Syria, and the latest conflict with Qatar. Speaking of Qatar, Saudi Arabia accuses Qatar of supporting terrorist groups, a statement I have reservations about given that 15 out of the 19 terrorists who attached New York and the Pentagon on 9/11 were Saudi nationals. As the translated Arabic adage goes, "the camel does not see his own hump." It behooves the Saudis to engage in some self-criticism and revisit various topics, including the interpretation of the Qur'an and tenets of Islam. Global-affairs analysts, intelligence and security analysts, and business leaders find it ironic that, following President Trump's visit to Saudi Arabia, in May 2017, the ultraconservative KSA embarks on more aggressive policies than the world has been accustomed to. For example, the perception is that President Trump's visit to Saudi Arabia gave the kingdom the green light to use unrestricted power to act, at its own discretion, regardless of international law, legal norms, and cultural traditions. The blockade of Qatar and the ongoing slaughter in Yemen exemplify how Saudi Arabia has abused that power. Its aggressive behavior raises many questions. Chief among them is whether the United States is willing to engage Iran militarily on behalf of Saudi Arabia. Is the United States willing to spill the blood of its soldiers and drain the financial resources of its hard-working citizens for causes that have nothing to do with America's interests? It is a dangerous path, to say the least, and President Trump needs to refrain from dangerous rhetoric because, in international relations, context matters. Mr. Trump needs to acquire the necessary political, social, religious, and cultural knowledge of the Middle East, a volatile region with ever-changing dynamics.

The other side of the same political coin is that Iran moves forward with its economic, political, and ideological aspirations in the region. The lifting of sanctions on Iran allows it to raise its international profile through economic ventures with China, Russia, Germany, and others. These economic ventures ultimately put pressure on Saudi Arabia's economy, leading the latter to reconsider its economic strategy when most, if not all, of its revenues depend heavily on oil. Now that oil prices are low, the KSA is forced to dip into its reserve funds. Shahine writes,

> Saudi Arabia's foreign reserves have dropped from a peak of more than $730 billion in 2014 after the plunge in oil prices, prompting the International Monetary Fund to warn that the kingdom may run out of financial assets needed to support spending within five years. Authorities have since embarked on an unprecedented plan to overhaul the economy and repair public finances.[7]

To demonstrate how the drop in oil prices has impacted the coffers in Saudi Arabia, one may look back at the example of the KSA's actions when it entered into an agreement to cut oil production with a non-OPEC member, Russia. The aim was to harm Iran economically—since it can sell oil on the open market following the lifting of sanctions—and to counter the ongoing decrease in oil prices. I do not expect oil prices to return to their pre-2014 prices of over $100 per barrel.

The international community also scrutinizes the Saudi royal family's covert internal power struggles after the elevation of prince MbS to crown prince, next in line to the throne. Undercover actions resulted in revelations of arrests and interrogations of deposed heirs, filling the pages of news outlets like the *Wall Street Journal*. The Saudis can no longer keep secret their internal squabbles. Now laid bare, those familial power struggles have worsened tensions within the KSA and have exacerbated anxieties throughout the international community over its present and future stability. Using history as my guide, I am reminded of the assassination of King Faisal on March 25, 1975, a rare example of how the royal family's internal fighting can spill over into the public square. This is problematic for two main reasons. First, MbS is young, impulsive, and lacks foreign-policy experience. Second, his military and economic policies in Yemen or Qatar proved to be disastrous. Similarly, the prince—who once vowed he would take his country's fight to Iran—forgets one of the first principles of international relations: Context matters. So, when MbS says that he will bring a war to Iran one day, then reaches out to them through Iraq the next day, it betrays his inability to fathom global affairs, regional politics, and the ramifications of escalating words of war.

Saudi Arabia is swimming in a sea of challenges it has never faced before, which raises two questions: Can Saudi Arabia be perceived as a regional power? Will it be able to affect the current political landscape in the Middle East? The answer to both questions is "no." I see no way that Saudi Arabia can limit Iran's growing influence in the region. America and Saudi Arabia no longer sit at the head of opposite ends of the meeting table. Those seats now belong to Russia and Iran. Subsequent pages address in greater depth how and why Saudi Arabia is increasing its economic and military ties with both China and Russia. Suffice it to say, the role the KSA has played in the region in the last 30 to 40 years is now nearly nonexistent.

The challenges the KSA faces seem to be too much to handle. The basis for my argument is that, through its ill-conceived policies, it has become evident that the KSA does not grasp the depth of the political paradigm shift in the Middle East. If the desert kingdom does, it seems unable to structure a well-defined strategy to address this shift. The ongoing failed military intervention in Yemen and the blockade on Qatar show evidence of this claim. Like many global-affairs analysts, Iranian officials do not know what to make of the KSA's continued failed policies. Do the failed policies suggest an internal struggle within the Saudi leadership or a breakdown in the decision-making process? Alternatively, do they reflect a rift over power with the elevation of MbS to crown prince, next in line to the throne? Whatever the case may be, the Saudi watchers conclude the role the KSA has played over the last three or four decades is ending.

In a volatile Middle East known for its turmoil and shifting loyalties, I wonder whether the United States, which maintained support for the desert kingdom for the last 70 years, will continue to support the KSA or change course. I believe American support will continue for years to come, but it will not be as extensive as it once was. For instance, will the United States fight another war in the Middle East on behalf of Saudi Arabia? The answer is "no." My reference is to President Trump's recent rhetoric over Iran. Questions are already emerging whether Washington hawks are pushing toward a military confrontation with Iran on Saudi Arabia's behalf. I strongly believe that the fiasco of the 2003 invasion of Iraq was based on lies advocated not only by Washington hawks, but also by Ahmed Chalabi, an Iraqi defector, code named "curveball." American citizens will not support another such undertaking.

If the United States ends up engaging Iran in war, I am convinced that Russia and China will support Iran behind the scenes. It is a dangerous path, to say the least. The other alternative announced by Mr. Trump is regime change in Iran. It not only demonstrates the president's ignorance about historical events (particularly ████████████████████ orchestrated-coup in support of the shah in 1953) but also what effect regime change will have on the political landscape of the region. Pursing a policy of regime change in Iran will fail now because the regional dynamics have changed from those of the 1950s when Mohamed Mosaddeq was successfully overthrown in favor of the shah. As we know, the 1979 Islamic Revolution in Iran later turned out to be a disaster that has changed the course of history.[8]

Under these sort of conditions, Washington hawks advocate forcibly for a war. The Kingdom of Saudi Arabia perceives the United States and its military as a tool to conduct wars on its behalf in return for a few billion dollars. Most defense, security, intelligence, and global-affairs analysts warn against trusting blindly or attending to the KSA's needs whenever it suits it. In the case of regime change, the stakes are high, and the outcome will be bad for the United States. In July 2017, Madison Schramm and Ariane M. Tabatabai argued, "Regime change, however, simply isn't feasible unless the United States is ready to commit, politically and militarily, to another Middle Eastern theater for an extended period of time."[9]

Even more concerning is President Trump's call for the cancellation of Iran's nuclear agreement. Even if the United States Congress agrees to such proposal, our allies in Europe will not. China and Russia will veto any proposal that would recommence international sanctions against Iran. Simply put, the United States will be going it alone while the Europeans, China, and Russia reap the economic benefits generated following the lifting of sanctions on Iran. I see no reason these countries will agree to reimpose sanctions on Iran just because the United States says so.

Precisely these dynamics, besides others, keep the Saudis guessing about Iranian intentions, actions, and future achievements. Iran is excited about its future global engagement possibilities, despite some limitations, because of its nuclear agreement with the West. These developments raise survival concerns within *the Saudi monarchy*, but also questions within *the international community* concerning the monarchy's stability. Yet, countries like Austria, Norway, Sweden, the United Kingdom, Germany, and Denmark expressed interest in investment opportunities in Iran. Denmark, for instance, proposed a $1 billion investment contribution to Iran's development plans.[10] I argue that Saudi Arabia's current strategy of choking and disrupting Iran's oil economy has failed miserably. Could this explain the KSA's recent outreach to Iraq to mediate the reestablishment of diplomatic ties between Riyadh and Tehran? Absolutely! For certain, the region's geopolitics favor Iran, not Saudi Arabia. The desert kingdom needs to accept that its regional leadership role is waning, its credibility is faltering, its Wahhabist ideology is under scrutiny, and its ability to influence oil prices is from a bygone era.

I. China-Saudi Arabia Relations

It is important to note that the China-Saudi Arabia relationship is for convenience and reciprocity on two fronts: economic and geopolitical. Saudi Arabia realizes that global wealth has begun to transfer from West to East; thus, the desert kingdom chooses to preposition itself for maximum benefit from the economic boom anticipated in Asia, led by China. Saudi Arabia's pivot toward China is driven by the political shift happening in the Middle East as much as it is driven by the economic opportunities that lie ahead. In a 2017 Reuters article, Ben Blanchard writes, "Saudi Arabia's King Salman oversaw the signing of deals worth as much as $65 billion on the first day of a visit to Beijing on Thursday, as the world's largest oil exporter looks to cement ties with the world's second-largest economy."[11]

Another reason the KSA decided to pivot toward China is Saudi Arabia's desire to undermine Iran's rapprochement with China after the former's nuclear agreement with the West. Interestingly, MbS wants to demonstrate to the world that he is a visionary and can turn his Vision 2030 into action—easier said than done given MbS's inexperience. Mohammed Bin Salman states:

> It is an ambitious yet achievable blueprint, which expresses our long-term goals and expectations and reflects our country's strengths and capabilities. All success stories start with a vision, and successful visions are based on strong pillars. The first pillar of our vision is our status as the heart of the Arab and Islamic worlds. We recognize that Allah the Almighty has bestowed on our lands a gift more precious than oil. Our Kingdom is the Land of the Two Holy Mosques, the most sacred sites on earth, and the direction of the Kaaba (Qibla) to which more than a billion Muslims turn at prayer...[12]

All things being equal, Saudi Arabia's oil richness interests China as fuel for its growing economy. As a result, China increased its economic cooperation with the Saudis both to ensure access to energy and to expand cooperation in defense and other areas. Minnie Chan writes, "A Chinese military website and military experts said Saudi Technology Development and Investment Company (TAQNIA) had signed a protocol with China's Aerospace Long-March International Trade (ALIT) for the drone production line at the biennial International Defence Exhibition and Conference (IDEX) in Abu Dhabi in February."[13] However, let us remember that the shifting political landscape in the Middle East is paving the way for China and Russia to increase their presence in the region. That shift includes (a) Iran's nuclear agreement with the West, which China and Russia strongly support; and (b) the ongoing civil war in Syria, regarding which China's UN Ambassador, Liu Jieyi, backed Russia's veto against the United Nations' call for a halt to bombing in the city of Aleppo, Syria.[14] Those actions highlight China's long-term strategy and send a message that China is in the Middle East to stay.

With this in mind, Saudi Arabia considers two main points: First, China's increased presence in the Middle East will significantly shape the region's political and economic landscape. Second, China and Iran's rapprochement *could* and *would* hinder the KSA's ability to influence, as it once did, the regional affairs of the Middle East. That influence is already faltering, and key players like Iran, Turkey, and Israel are taking notice. Similarly, major powers realize that Saudi Arabia's ability to influence events on the ground is becoming more and more limited. Could Saudi Arabia's recent overture to Iraq to mend relations between Riyadh and Tehran stem from fear? Possibly! The fear would be that, if China and Russia keep cooperating and improving ties with Iran—I believe they will—the outcome could hurt the Saudis in the long run. The other explanation is that the Saudis realize that the international community's lifting of sanctions on Iran allows the latter to flood the market with oil. Iran, after all, is the 4th-largest oil-producing country, and the presence of its oil on the international market would in turn decrease revenues for Saudi Arabia. Chen Aizhu notes that China's oil imports from Iran have increased enormously since January 2017: "Chinese firms were expected to lift between 3 million to 4 million barrels more Iranian oil each quarter in 2017 than last year, four sources with knowledge of the matter estimated. That would be about 5 percent to 7 percent higher than the 620,000 barrels per day (bpd) of Iranian crude the country has imported during the first 11 months of 2016, according to the customs data."[15]

While closely watching political developments in the Middle East is an endless undertaking, China sees cooperation with Saudi Arabia from a different perspective. From an economic viewpoint, China reasons that it makes sense to secure access to energy from two top oil producers in the region (Iran and the KSA) to support its economic machinery. This undertaking will likely continue for many years. Thus, China is thinking that persistent chaos in the Middle East and enduring tensions between Riyadh and Tehran guarantee access to oil through either Saudi Arabia, Iran, or both. There is a counter argument, which I am certain Chinese policymakers have considered. China leaves itself open to major security and economic vulnerabilities by increasing and deepening its reliance on oil from the Middle East. That strategy could prove detrimental.[16]

What about the future? China and Saudi Arabia's relations will continue as long as the economic cooperation serves both countries' interests. Subsequent pages address this cooperation in more detail and highlight how China, not Saudi Arabia, stands to benefit from this relationship.

II. Russia-Saudi Arabia Relations

Who would have thought that the time would come for the world to witness cooperation between Russia and Saudi Arabia after almost a half-century of mutual suspicion and, frankly, political hostility behind the scenes? Moreover, how could we forget the images of Mujahedeen in Afghanistan supported and financed by Saudi Arabia and trained by the United States fighting the USSR after its invasion of Afghanistan, in 1979? Yet, in the volatile Middle East, Riyadh resumed its diplomatic ties with Moscow and went beyond political niceties to include defense and energy discussions. Talk about change! I refer to the meeting that took place in the Kremlin when then-prince Saud al Faisal, the Saudi foreign minister, solicited the support of President Mikhail S. Gorbachev against Iraq's seizure of Kuwait in the 1990s. Fast-forward to today: Russia and Saudi Arabia find themselves far apart on issues like Iran, Syria, and Yemen. Yet, both countries—Russia and Saudi Arabia—cooperate despite these basic differences. Like China before it, Russia perceives its cooperative relationship with Saudi Arabia as one of suitability and convenience, with no strategic aspirations on the horizon.

Before elaborating further, let us review a historical snapshot of key information that shaped relations between Russia and Saudi Arabia over the past thirty-five-plus years. A major incident occurred in the 1980s

13

with the Soviet Union's invasion of Afghanistan. As an OPEC member, Saudi Arabia decided to singlehandedly triple oil production at that time, thus crashing world oil prices and bankrupting the Soviet Union. That move served to punish the then-USSR. Interestingly, the geopolitical tables have turned. As the Syrian civil war emerged on the global stage, Russia intervened in the conflict, for geopolitical reasons that go beyond the borders of the Middle East. It continues to ship military hardware to Syria, provide the Syrian regime with air cover, and deploy troops and advanced fighter jets to the Syrian theater. While the Saudis have vehemently echoed their desire for the removal of Bashar al-Assad from power, Russia insists that any talks regarding peace in Syria must involve the current president al-Assad. Russia even used its veto power at the United Nations Security Council (UNSC) against any resolution for international military intervention. It was Russia's way of telling the world that Moscow runs the show in the Syrian theater. Despite all this, somehow Russia and Saudi Arabia decided to move their cooperation forward to include economic and military ventures. While this cooperation included different sectors, the focus is mainly on energy given the drop in oil prices. This cooperation accelerated due to not only the sharp drop in the international oil market, but also Iran's agreement with the West over its nuclear program. Gemma Acton writes, "The Middle Eastern kingdom has enjoyed a longstanding and broadly cooperative relationship with the U.S., dating back to the start of oil exploration within Saudi Arabia in the 1930s. The latest cast of key characters, headed by U.S. President Donald Trump and Saudi's King Salman, has established a warmer rapport than seen during the final years of former President Barack Obama's presidency when tensions developed over Saudi Arabia's stance on Iran and Yemen."[17]

Like China, Russia fully understands that its cooperation with Saudi Arabia, a staunch US ally, is short lived and will not transform into a strategic alliance—not by any stretch of the imagination. Moscow realizes the persistent chaos in the Middle East as it dictates the agenda, sometimes openly, sometimes behind the scenes. Moscow recognizes enduring tensions between Iran and Saudi Arabia and witnesses the continuing decline of the United States' involvement in the region. I believe that Russia aims for a far greater role in the Middle East in view of the previously mentioned developments. For instance, the rift between Saudi Arabia and

Iran illustrates the need for Russia to preposition itself—and it already has—by supporting both Iran (nuclear agreement with the West) and Syria (ongoing civil war), thus allowing Russia's reentry into the region through much wider doors.[18]

The Russian International Affairs Council (RIAC) claims that the Russian-Saudi relations are strategic in nature; that claim is subject to further debate. Russia will have to do a lot more than invest in the energy sector or decide on oil prices in cooperation with the Saudis. Rather, Russia needs to offer Riyadh services such as nuclear energy or aerospace technology that other countries in the Middle East cannot acquire, thus providing Saudi Arabia greater strategic capabilities. The Saudis *have* the financial means to make such purchases. Sometimes, however, funding alone is not enough for a new industry to take off or guarantee its success. Grigory Kosach writes, "However, in order to secure positions on the Saudi market, Russia will need ingenuity and the ability to offer competitive products and services in various areas, such as space, nuclear power engineering, agriculture, etc. Another promising area for cooperation is the provision of Russia's services to facilitate the establishment of the Saudi defence sector, including on the basis of cooperation with other contracting parties."[19]

I disagree with the claim that Russia and Saudi Arabia are destined for a strategic alliance. There are major issues like the Arab-Israeli conflict, the status of Jerusalem, Iran, Syria, Yemen, and Libya among others that Russia and Saudi Arabia do not see eye to eye on and must address. Further, should Saudi Arabia align its policy with whatever Russia is advocating in Syria, for instance? If so, the KSA risks alienating itself from the Muslim world even more. I believe that Saudi Arabia cannot afford to take such a position and is therefore unwilling to support such a policy given its waning role in the greater Middle East and the Muslim world, writ large.

Subsequent pages detail where I anticipate the relationships will go and how they may develop given the geopolitical shift in the Middle East, Iran's growing influence, Turkey's assertive foreign policy, Egypt's security and political chaos, Syria's ongoing civil war, and Yemen's upheavals, among others.

III. US-Saudi Arabia Relations

Chapter 5 is devoted to US-Saudi relations. This section produces a snapshot of what this relationship entails. Mention the Middle East in conversation nowadays, and one hears the cliché that everything hinges on US-Saudi relations. That is understandable: over decades, the two countries have cooperated on issues of either energy (mainly oil) or regional policy (support of one group or country over another). This relationship recalls the 1930s and the era of oil discovery, which changed the trajectory of US-Saudi relations. That era witnessed a sea of changes that still serve the strategic and security interests of both countries. Could this relationship stand the test of time? Was it destined to last forever? Many analysts in defense, security, business, energy, and global affairs are asking these questions given the changing narrative in the greater Middle East. These questions also underscore the main issue on which, I believe, the US-Saudi relationship was—and still is—based. That issue is *oil in return for security.* The KSA made sure to give the United States unlimited access to lower priced oil. This basic economic arrangement made cooperation possible in other areas such as defense and intelligence sharing. However, the events of September 11, 2001, proved that both players, at times, cherry picked the intelligence they would share, depending on each intelligence agency's policy objectives; this theme receives attention in the subsequent pages. For now, suffice it to say, both the United States and Saudi Arabia serve each other's interests.

Events in the Middle East, over the past 70 years, never cease to amaze an outsider. In the volatile Middle East, the US-Saudi relationship had to adapt to changes, ranging from the rise of nationalism under Jamal Abd Al-Nasser and the B'ath party in Syria and Iraq, to the Iran Islamic Revolution and the Iran-Iraq War. Yet, it is the policies of Iran—the archenemy of Saudi Arabia—that Washington and Riyadh continue to converge over. One notices how upset Saudi Arabia was with the United States when it, along with other major powers and Germany (known as P5+1), reached an agreement with Iran over its nuclear program. Saudi Arabia's displeasure of the agreement was evident. Yet, the KSA managed to contain its disapproval of the deal and not draw criticism from within the Muslim world as to why KSA is siding with a non-Muslim country (the US) against a Muslim one (Iran). Alia Chughtai and Hala Saadani write, "While today there seems to be a strategic alignment between Saudi Arabia's interests in the region and those of the US, mostly centering around controlling Iran's regional reach, there have been low points in this relationship that were brought about by major events. Saudi Arabia has always sought balance between its role as a leader in the Arab world and its strong ties to the US."[20]

The present work allocates an entire chapter to the US-Saudi relations under each US administration from Truman to Trump. This section highlights the overall thinking of the US government on Saudi Arabia. Note, during the Obama administration, the tense US-Saudi relations and how they exposed an array of differences, especially concerning Iran's nuclear program. Yemen was another contentious issue the Obama administration clashed over with the Saudis. As Saudi Arabia was putting together a coalition of Arab countries to support its military intervention against the Houthi rebels in Yemen, who had taken over the capital, Sanaa, the Obama administration warned Riyadh about civilian casualties resulting from military engagement in Yemen. It turned out the Obama administration offered the right assessment. Reports from the United Nations and current news coming out of Yemen suggest that the conflict left *18 million* people desperately needing humanitarian assistance since Saudi Arabia's invasion of Yemen. Many experts categorize the resulting food scarcity as the largest food security emergency in the world.[21]

Positive attitudes, however short lived, took different directions in Riyadh and Washington once President Trump was sworn in. How ironic! Before becoming president, Trump sternly criticized Saudi Arabia, directing harsh words at the KSA: "the US should not be working to support Saudi terrorists." All this was water under the bridge when President Trump took his first foreign trip to none other than Saudi Arabia. Was it the president's way of saying, "I'm sorry"? Did the president's first foreign foray betray his awkward grasp of foreign affairs? Whatever the case may be, it became evident that the trip President Trump made to Saudi Arabia served the latter's interests *very* well. My reference is to how, given Trump's lack of credibility, garbled messages, inconsistencies, and bashing of Muslims, the Muslim world received his speech in Riyadh with low expectations. The speech was less about the Muslim world and more geared toward Iran.

How convenient it was for the Saudis to have the American president speak on their behalf about issues that they should deal with themselves. In my opinion, the trip failed. Rather than confront the Muslim world (mainly its leaders) on its double standards, oppression, lack of freedom of expression, and human rights abuses, Trump made it possible for Arab and Muslim leaders to continue their abuses and atrocities. Atrocities committed under the pretext of terrorism in countries like Egypt, Algeria, Saudi Arabia, Iraq, United Arab Emirates, and Bahrain were implicitly condoned. Alas, Mr. Trump truly missed a historic opportunity. J. Weston Phippen writes:

> Leaders at the meeting seemed optimistic that Trump would bring change and opportunity. Some have previously complained that former-President Obama offered little decisive action and moralized too much. Trump, instead, has made it clear that he will not criticize Middle East countries for their humanitarian abuses. Earlier in the trip, Trump met with the King of Bahrain, Hamad bin Isa al-Khalifa, whose country recently approved a constitutional change that allows its military court to try civilians. The move was an effort to contain growing unrest, and human rights organizations have greatly objected to the decision. The Trump administration has stayed quiet, and even signaled it would lift humanitarian restrictions on Bahrain that curtailed the sale of F-16 fighter jets and other military arms to the country.[22]

The United States is no longer able to play its traditional role as a guarantor of stability in the greater Middle East, a role it had played since World War II. How has the United States lost that role? It says one thing and does another. It is time for the United States to conduct a top to bottom review of its foreign policy toward the Middle East. It is time for the US to evaluate its relations with regional countries that have depended on it for their survival in the last half-century. As the geopolitical shift in the Middle East ensues, the United States needs to reevaluate its policy of supporting Saudi Arabia, the world's largest exporter of oil, the place of Islam's holiest sites, and a country equally bountiful in advanced American weapons and furious Wahhabi Sunni Muslims. Similarly, Saudi Arabia—and the Muslim world, for that matter—need to stop playing the "victim card." And how could misguided Muslims claim that Prophet Muhammed is a mercy to mankind when Asiya Bibi, Youssef Naderkhani and Lena Joy, among others, have been charged with blasphemy and apostasy and sentenced to death?[23] Muslim scholars and leaders alike, conveniently or ignorantly, have left an important fact out of the debate. Apostasy and blasphemy laws are not rooted in Islam but are driven *solely* by ignorance and legalistic guile.

Let us put this claim within the context of President Trump's visit to Saudi Arabia in May 2017 by considering the role of the Wahhabist ideology. Wahhabism is the guiding religious force in Saudi Arabia. The desert kingdom now spreads Wahhabism worldwide thanks to its petrodollars! We have seen Wahhabism in Afghanistan with the Taliban, in the Philippines with Abu Sayyaf, and in Somalia with Al-Shabab. Consider the influence of the Saudi Wahhabist ideology in Pakistan: the increased numbers of religious madrassas is staggering. For instance, in 1947, there were 250 madrassas. In 1987, they increased to 3,000, and, in 2008, there were over 40,000 madrassas.[24] President Trump should have used his speech in Saudi Arabia to highlight issues of great concern to the Muslim world: reform of the educational system, freedom of the press, freedom of expression, women's rights, and so forth.[25]

Major challenges lie ahead for the United States in its relationship with the Kingdom of Saudi Arabia. I am not naïve—this relationship will not change overnight. It has evolved over decades, and it will most likely take decades for it to dissipate. However, the emergence of new players in the Middle East like Russia, China, and Iran gives me pause to rethink the "what ifs." These new players have military strength, act shrewdly in diplomatic matters, and possess the economic might to woo some regional countries to their camp, thereby changing the geopolitical calculus for everyone.

As I argued in my previous book, *Volatile State: Iran in the Nuclear Age*, the failure of American foreign policy in the Middle East can be attributed to a host of issues that include its ill-defined strategy; lack of cultural, social, and historical understanding of the region; and foreign-policy double standards approach. Against this backdrop, other countries in the Middle East and elsewhere are realizing that keeping the United

States entangled in a chaotic Middle East is the best strategy. One does not have to fight the Americans in a war. Rather, let the Americans drain their economic resources as they did in Iraq and are still doing in Afghanistan.

The shifting geopolitical landscape of the Middle East compels both the United States and Saudi Arabia to reorient their focus. The KSA has already begun that process by shifting away from the US toward China for two main reasons. First, Saudi Arabia realizes that the US is increasing its own oil production, resulting in less American demand. Second, wealth is transferring from the West to the East in the wake of China's economic preeminence. That presents huge economic opportunities for the KSA to benefit from. On the other hand, the United States is politically handicapped to do anything in the Middle East, as policymakers in Washington are marred in political infighting while Americans suffer from a leadership crisis. The world gets the message regarding the chaotic state of affairs inside the US government. Clearly, Riyadh plans to keep the United States as a backup plan for when intrigues, from without or from within, threaten the survival of the Saudi monarchy.

IV. Royal Family Infighting over Power

Most historians agree that Saudi Arabia's history is marked by decades of internal struggles over kingly succession among royal family members who form opposing factions. An outsider who is unfamiliar with the history of Saudi Arabia or the nature of its tribal mentality may struggle to understand the succession battles happening within the Saudi royal palace. First, and by way of preface, the royal family is estimated at about 15,000 members. However, a smaller number of about 2,000 hold most of the power and wealth. This smaller group requires absolute allegiance from the rest and has no interest in compromise. In the kingdom's history, two succession events have occurred through assassination. The first came when Faisal Ibn Turki passed the kingdom to his son Abdullah Ibn Faisal Ibn Turki between 1785 and 1865. The second assassination happened when Prince Faisal bin Musaed bin Abdelaziz, 27 years old at the time, shot his uncle, King Faisal, in 1975.[26] His son, Crown Prince Khalid, succeeded the latter to the throne. The causes of the assassination of King Faisal remain unknown.

In fact, until recently, the world rarely heard about Saudi royal palace intrigues. Assassinations are, to be sure, aberrations and demand attention in the pages of history. Nevertheless, pulling back the curtain on those dark chapters of the KSA's history sheds light on the unusual scenes taking place inside the royal palace today. Succession in Saudi Arabia transitions from brother to brother. Allegiance controls the process. King Abdulaziz, the founder of the Kingdom of Saudi Arabia, introduced the rules of succession, and subsequent Saudi kings adhered to those customs until the current king, Salman, ended the protocol. The latter elevated his son, MbS, to crown prince and next in line to the throne, in June 2017. One does not have to look far to see the subsequent uncertainty within the Saudi royal family. Yet, for decades to come, MbS's elevation changes the KSA's future. MbS is young, 32 as of this writing. When he ascends to the throne—assuming he will not be challenged or assassinated—he will rule for the next forty to fifty years. However, one must remain mindful that the rule of the crown prince, MbS, may be rejected by other royal family members, some of whom show allegiance to the deposed crown prince, Mohammed bin Nayef (MbN).

MbS is inexperienced. Thirty-two is a young age to bear the burdens of rulership. Crown Prince MbS has much to learn about global affairs, the impact of bellicose words and outright threats—like the ones he delivered to Iran. MbS fancies that wars can be easy. He advocated for invading Yemen to defeat the Houthi rebels only to find the action hasty and without an exit strategy. Now, the KSA is mired in Yemen, accused of killing civilians (Muslims) and creating a countrywide famine. The young crown prince seems unable to learn the lessons of history or think things through rationally and pragmatically. Subsequent pages consider whether Washington has nodded its approval to MbS's promotion.[27]

Impromptu succession tactics—replacing one prince with another or otherwise preferring to promote one over another—do not happen in a vacuum. A hidden force, behind the scenes, often steers succession according to the agenda of the sitting king, revealing his hopes and wishes. I predict that when King Salman, 82 as of this writing, dies, hostility toward his son, crown prince MbS, will follow. In that case, watch for royal supporters of MbN, the deposed crown prince, to conspire to undermine the young king's authority. Such circumstances among the royal family members could even lead to a horrific outcome: assassination. Hugh Miles, freelance journalist in the *Guardian*, writes: "The letters in Arabic calling for the overthrow of the king have been read more than 2m times. The letters call on the 13 surviving sons of Ibn Saud—specifically the princes Talal, Turki and Ahmed bin Abdulaziz—to unite and remove the leadership in a palace coup, before choosing a new government from within the royal family. 'Allow the oldest and most capable to take over the affairs of the state, let the new king and crown prince take allegiance from all, and cancel the strange, new rank of second deputy premier,' states the first letter."[28]

Should he take power as planned, the inexperienced, impulsive prince, MbS, will deal moreover with the religious establishment. Will he bow to the ultraconservative religious establishment, or will he challenge its authority? Will he uphold the twisted interpretation of Islam on a host of issues (girls' education, women's rights, etc.)? Alternatively, will he advocate for a tolerable tone to the interpretation of the Qur'an? The world has wised up to and begun to scrutinize the Saudis' harsh Wahhabist interpretation of the Qur'an. Consider, for example, that Wahhabist interpretations of Islam have contributed to 9/11, turning countries like Afghanistan, Chechnya, Nigeria, Somalia, Iraq, Syria, and Libya into hotbeds of extremism and intolerance. I doubt that MbS can control the religious establishment. Even challenging the influence of the Saudi religious establishment, in place since the inception of the desert kingdom, will be like setting foot on a bed of hot coals. Nevertheless, the crown prince must find a way to deal with increasing international investigation, and that may be only through the very trial by fire that he is at pains to avoid.

Whatever the outcome, King Salman, who ascended to the throne in 2015, will be remembered as the sovereign who altered the course of Saudi Arabian history by redrawing the kingdom's lines of succession. His strategy virtually assures an internal power struggle among the royal family members. On the one hand, some will advocate for concentrating power in the hands of MbS. On the other hand, some will sabotage the new king and quietly—or openly—revolt against him. Such dissension could bring the demise of the Kingdom of Saudi Arabia as we know it. This claim may sound hyperbolic. Nevertheless, King Salman ended an age-old decree, issued by King Abdulaziz, founding sovereign of Saudi Arabia, that the kingship should pass from brother to brother. Had rescinding the decree opened the door for elections in Saudi Arabia, it may have resonated with the international community *at least*. Yet, the new decree bespeaks merely another monarchial manipulation, an individual king's wishes for succession made reality. After such arbitrariness and disregard of custom, one should *expect* the KSA to descend into chaos as in the eras of assassinations that marked the dark chapters of its history. Subsequent pages offer a detailed account of how conflicts over kingship in Saudi Arabia will only intensify, leading to questions about the kingdom's stability and the monarchy's survival.

V. Saudi Arabia's Wahhabism Ideology

Saudi Arabia embraces a Wahhabist ideology and propagates it worldwide, to further its political agenda. Saudi Arabia's petrodollars have allowed it to spread the ideology, which is based on a deviant interpretation of Islam. Thus, Wahhabism has gained ground and much influence in some Muslim countries, including Afghanistan, Pakistan, Nigeria, and Somalia. The KSA spreads the ideology also by using its religious status as the birthplace of Islam and home to the two holiest sites of the Islamic faith: Mecca and Medina.

Yet, Wahhabism has always been about two things: (a) spreading an ascetic lifestyle (one that I believe has nothing to do with Islam); and (b) making sure no other religious school of thought challenges its authority, which is both self-justifying and based on flimsy religious leadership. How ironic, amusing, and hypocritical to hear the grand Mufti of Saudi Arabia, Abdulaziz Ibn Abdullah Abdullatif—who is *appointed* by the king, *must* embrace the Wahhabism ideology, and avidly advocates the warped creed—speak of Saudi Arabia fighting terrorism. The grand Mufti's words are like putting an Islamic rubber stamp on a statement to give it legitimacy. After all, the statements come from the *birthplace* of Islam; thus, they *must* be credible, logical, and true. It is nonsense, to say the least! "The Grand Mufti of Saudi Arabia, condemned Islamic State of Iraq and the Levant (Isil), insisting the ideas of extremism, radicalism and terrorism do not belong to Islam in any way. Somewhat paradoxically, however, members of the Saudi ruling class have applauded Wahhabism for its Salafi piety, i.e. its adherence to the original practices of Islam and the movement's vehement opposition to the Shia branch of Islam."[29] How could statements like the ones the grand mufti issued be accurate when considering that fifteen out of the nineteen terrorists who attacked New York and the Pentagon on 9/11 were Saudi nationals? Alas, the Wahhabist ideology has extended into the far corners of the Muslim world from Pakistan and Afghanistan to Somalia and Sudan. Forget about engaging in a dialogue about the lies and perverse interpretations promoted by Wahhabism, let alone questioning the religion of Islam.[30]

Subsequent pages present a detailed account of the Wahhabist ideology as part of Saudi Arabia's identity and foreign-policy tool. However, this chapter's narrative limits itself to developing key themes only. Readers must have a clear picture of the path Saudi Arabia uncovered and on which it spreads its perverted ideology, claiming that it represents the pure version of Islam. Based on my research and familiarity with the culture and the religion of Islam, the KSA's statements are far from the truth. Highlighting how Wahhabism spread like a wildfire is well deserving of an explanation.

It all started in the 1970s when the Saudi royal leadership diverted some of its petrodollars into promoting Wahhabism in the Muslim world. Saudi charities funneled money into establishing religious schools, known as "Madrassas" (a softer version for Wahhabi schools). These religious schools grew immensely: madrassas were being established in rural areas of Pakistan, Afghanistan, the Philippines, Indonesia, Nigeria, Somalia, Algeria, Egypt, and Malaysia. It was a global project of a global outreach facilitated by Saudi Arabia's vast petrodollar largesse. Interestingly, estimations of the dollar amounts Saudi Arabia spent on spreading Wahhabism vary from one country to another. For instance, Great Britain opined that an estimated excess of $100 billion dollars was spent exporting fanatical Wahhabism to poorer Muslim nations worldwide.[31] Similarly, the US State Department has estimated that, over the past four decades, Riyadh has invested more than $10 billion dollars into charitable foundations in an attempt to replace mainstream Sunni Islam with Wahhabism. European Union (EU) intelligence experts estimate that 15 to 20 percent of this amount—$100 billion—has been diverted to al-Qaida and other violent jihadists.[32] My argument about the danger of Wahhabism has less to do with its origins or its past; it has more to do with its itinerary and long-term objectives.

Those who have been following the development of this dangerous ideology know that it "takes two to tango." Wahhabism has a dance partner, so to speak. In the last three or four decades, the West has obliged. Wahhabism could not have achieved what it has without the support of the West, which, from time to time, ignored the warning signs. The United States bears as much responsibility as the Kingdom of Saudi Arabia for supporting and allowing the spread of Wahhabism. Saudi Arabia's long-term vision to spread Wahhabism merged well with the United States' efforts, in the 1970s, to defeat Communism. It got even better for both when the Soviet Union made the mistake of invading Afghanistan, in 1979. As a result, Washington and Riyadh concluded that they could achieve their separate objectives together. The Saudis funded the Americans, who trained the Mujahedeen. Interestingly, one Saudi official, Prince Turki bin Faisal al-Saud, oversaw the US-Saudi relations from an intelligence perspective, especially in Afghanistan. He developed strong ties with the Central Intelligence Agency while maintaining his relationship with Osama Bin Laden and other fighters in Afghanistan.[33] What a great way for the United States to merge its agenda (defeat the Soviet Union) with that of Saudi Arabia (spread Wahhabism). At least that was the thinking back then. The 9/11 attacks on New York and the Pentagon, however, proved that Washington's short-term gains over long-term strategy were a miscalculated policy. Anahita Hamzei writes:

> Poor, rural areas were first introduced to the Wahhabi Cult dogma—outside of Saudi Arabia; they were shadowed as the next of regions on a long list to implement strict, intolerant, fascist Wahhabi ideology: Saudi's plans happened to coalesce with US government's intent to combat the Soviet Union in the 1970's. Afghanistan had been invaded and occupied in the midst of the Cold War by the Soviet Union. Coincidently, USA's agendas amalgamated with that of Saudi Arabia's; henceforth, they became greater allies in supporting the indoctrination

of Wahhabi ideologies (7). The Wahhabi initiative commenced as planned. Training and conditioning through Wahhabi-centered manuscript and literature, funded by Saudi Arabia's "charitable" printing press, took off as an extensive campaign in this region. USA, by way of CIA and other secretive military operations, took part in promoting Wahhabi doctrine to raise a strong "Mujahidin" front with their Saudi partners in fascism.[34]

I am not naïve to think that writing a few pages about Wahhabism will delegitimize it in the eyes of Muslim adherents—those who embrace such thinking around the world—or turn it to a useless, baseless, and unfounded ideology. Nor will an outsider to the Islamic faith be competent to change course by challenging the religious notions and concepts of Wahhabist ideology that have been drilled into the minds of Muslims for decades. Thus far, Wahhabism has achieved its objective—the application of an ascetic lifestyle based on a misguided interpretation of the Qur'an and basic tenets of Islam. Muhammad Ne'ma Al-Semawi writes, "The Wahhabis justify their brutish actions with the alleged goal of purifying the Arabian Peninsula and the rest of the world from the unbelievers, even though their violence has no basis in traditional Islamic texts, such as the Quran."[35]

One does not have to look far to realize what is taking place in remote areas of Waziristan and Rawalpindi, Pakistan; Qandahar, Afghanistan; or Mogadishu, Somalia. I wonder if Muslims will ever question, as they should, where their faith is headed given Saudi Arabia's ongoing promotion of Wahhabism. Do everyday Muslims wonder why Islam is stuck, unable to evolve as Christianity has through two thousand years of history? Contributing to this lack of progress is, unsurprisingly, a dissimulating debate in which pleasantries obscure atrocities like honor killings, the prevention of girls from attending schools, and blasphemy. Based on my understanding of the religion, Islam never advocates nor promotes atrocities.

Some officials in western capitals argue that elements or countries other than the Saudis cause extremism in Islam. Consider, for example, the argument of Lt. Gen. Thomas McInerney, a retired US Air Force General and defense industry executive, who states, "What I don't like about this is (that) the number one leading radical Islamic group in the world is the Iranians. They are purveyors of radical Islam throughout the region and throughout the world." I respectfully disagree with Lt. Gen. McInerney, who cherry picked his facts. To say that Iran, for instance, uses terrorism as a tool of its foreign policy, a claim with which I agree, is to refrain from telling the whole truth: that Saudi Arabia's Wahhabism has been linked to terrorism.[36]

VI. Conclusion

This chapter's objective has been to show the framework for my arguments, arguments established on facts, rationality, and truth. It will not do the readers justice if I cherry pick information or promote one side of the argument over another. Rather, I present the argument as it is and let readers reach their own conclusions. In the case of the Wahhabist ideology, I believe it is time to ask the hard questions, to scrutinize who is behind the funding of this perverted creed, behind this extremism within the Muslim world. However, when I read and hear some experts arguing that Iran, not Saudi Arabia, for instance, is the *only* threat to the region—the *only* threat to the United States, for that matter—I must reprove those critics for having chosen to be dishonest to themselves and to their audience. Their dishonesty requires a response!

The following sections address in great depth the historical events that have made Saudi Arabia what it is today. I also address its sources of power, which come mainly from petrodollars and religion. Yet, those sources are shrinking as time goes by. More and more, Saudi Arabia is becoming irrelevant given (a) Iran's growing influence in the Middle East, (b) Saudi royal internal struggles over succession to kingship, and (c) shifts unfavorable to Saudi Arabia in the geopolitical landscape of the region.

Make no mistake: Saudi Arabia will fight hard to sustain its leadership—whatever is left of it—in the Muslim world. The odds favor the desert kingdom for one important reason: two of the holiest sites in Islam, Mecca and Medina, are there. Those two sites are good fortune and reason enough for the Saudis to play hardball.

CHAPTER II

History of Saudi Arabia: Past and Present

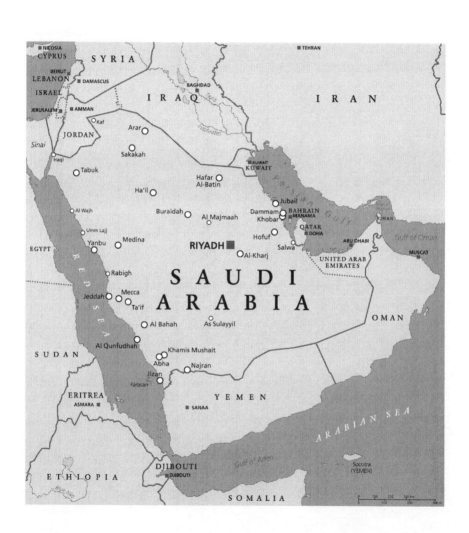

Introduction

Before writing further about the Kingdom of Saudi Arabia, one must define the conservative monarchy's geographical territory and place its geography within the context of modern-day Saudi Arabia. Afterward, readers will better understand Saudi Arabia's foreign-policy pursuits. My explanation and examination also address the ongoing international scrutiny that Saudi Arabia has undergone since the latest WikiLeaks information suggested that Saudi Arabia has funded terrorism and funds it to this day. Nevertheless, without first becoming acquainted with the historical background in which Saudi Arabia got its territory and expanded its influence, readers would find it challenging to understand why today's Saudi Arabia behaves as it does.

A brief, admittedly selective description follows of Saudi Arabia's history, geography, religion, demographics, and foreign relations. All those factors combined to transform the desert kingdom from a nomadic tribe into an influential country. Throughout centuries, those characteristics shaped Saudi Arabia into what it is today. This chapter begins, then, with a narrative of Saudi Arabia's historical identity.

One can cover the history of Saudi Arabia in a few pages. It began as a cluster of nomadic tribes spread throughout the Arabian Peninsula. People may find it a challenging proposition to decipher the early civilization of the Arabian Peninsula where Saudi Arabia had a recorded presence there. Indeed, the West suffers from the unfortunately persistent misconception that Islam was born in Saudi Arabia. The Islamic faith originated in 610 AD, but the KSA was established more than a millennium later, in 1932. Located on a small part of a peninsula in Southwest Asia, the land that is now Saudi Arabia was part of a region that served, over the centuries, as an ancient trade center and the birthplace of Islam. Saudi Arabia was well positioned, geographically, to influence events to its benefit. The discovery of oil accelerated Saudi Arabia's transition from a desert tribe into a global player, primarily, in the energy sector. Subsequent pages address that role in detail.

Early History of Saudi Arabia

Knowing the early history of the desert kingdom, especially in its pre-Islamic era, could help one better understand modern-day Saudi Arabia. However, I do not intend to detail how the early historical record of human presence in the Arabian Peninsula, which dates back some 15,000 to 20,000 years, has shaped and influenced the KSA's trajectory. Survival depended mainly on hunting and gathering as humans roamed the vast swaths of land on the Arabian Peninsula. During the last period of the Ice Age, the European ice cap started to melt. The resultant rising temperatures rendered the peninsula a hot, arid land.

Today, of course, the world thinks first of that hot, dry climate when it thinks of the Middle East. Yet, many do not realize that, before the Ice Age, lush grasslands covered the peninsula, and oases attracted human migrants to the region. Lifestyles evolved from solely depending on hunting and gathering to developing other means of survival. Agriculture, for example, developed first in Mesopotamia, then in the Nile River Valley, and eventually spread across the Middle East.[37] The domestication of agriculture brought new ideas. Historical records, for instance, indicate that pottery allowed farmers to store their food. The domestication of animals like goats, camels, and horses proved equally important. It provided the settlers not only with a source of revenue, but also with further means of survival. After developing those new methods of survival, local settlers abandoned hunting and focused on the perfecting agriculture and animal husbandry. Economic and social changes resulted, making possible semipermanent settlements and laying the foundations of society, politics, culture, and architecture. Those changes were the building blocks of what people know today as Middle Eastern culture. Characteristic of that culture is a mix of different ethnicities, languages, customs, and religious beliefs. This observation leads to a broader discussion of the Arabian Peninsula.

Those unfamiliar with the role the Arabian Peninsula has played throughout history should note that this part of the world lay between two great centers of civilization: the Nile River Valley and Mesopotamia. Thus, the region had both geographical and strategic significance. This crossroads location gave the region a trade advantage. As such, the Arabian

Peninsula was not a volatile place, but a lifeline for the whole region, which populated later. Thus, the peninsula became an intersection of major trade routes for transporting agricultural goods highly sought after in Mesopotamia, the Nile Valley, and the Mediterranean Basin.[38] The trade routes provided a passage for large caravans to cross swaths of the lands known today as Oman and Yemen. Interestingly, the caravans crossed through Saudi Arabia's Asir Province and then through what is today Makkah (aka Mecca) and Medina: two large and important cities in Saudi Arabia.

Now think of this bustling commercial center in approximately 610 AD. At that time, the city of Mecca, one of the commercial centers of the region, was home to Muhammed, who will become the prophet. At that time, Muhammed began to receive revelations from Allah (God) through the Angel Gabriel to claim God's oneness. The revelations caused a tremendous growth of fellowship and marked the birth of Islam. However, the inhabitants did not initially receive the Prophet Muhammed's message well. He learned of an assassination plot against him and decided to migrate, along with his followers, to Yathrib, later named Madinat Al-Nabi (the City of the Prophet) and now named Medina. Some Muslim countries in the Middle East, including Saudi Arabia, base their yearly calendar on this event—the migration to Yathrib. After Muhammed's migration, many battles took place between the followers of the Prophet Muhammed and the pagans of Mecca. Prophet Muhammed, however, unified the tribes around 628, according to historical record. A mere century after Islam's birth, the Islamic empire extended from Seville of the Andalusia region in Spain to parts of India and China. Yet, despite the large territories acquired by the Islamic empire, the Arabian Peninsula did not serve as its political epicenter; rather, the peninsula remained the main trade center.

Trade encouraged visitors, merchants, and pilgrims to visit the peninsula. Some of those visitors decided to settle in Mecca and Medina. Ideas, culture, and customs exchanged subsequently between the peninsula and other civilizations. While interacting with each other, people needed a common language in order to communicate. Consequently, the Arabic language became not only the medium whereby Arab and Muslims communicated, but also a basis of learning and, specifically, of acquiring scientific knowledge.

Before proceeding further, let us briefly clarify the difference between an Arab and a Muslim. Many in the West have a hard time distinguishing between the two. To this day, western audiences assume that a Muslim is an Arab and an Arab is a Muslim, and the terms *Arab* and *Muslim* are frequently used interchangeably. That usage is mistaken. An Arab is an individual whose ancestry originated in the Arabian Peninsula. A Muslim is an individual who embraces the religion of Islam. According to those criteria, the Prophet Muhammed was an Arab since he was born in the Arabian Peninsula, and he was the founder of Islam, a Muslim. However, an Arab need not be a Muslim. An Arab can be of any religious faith, including Judaism, Christianity, and Islam.

Now, here are some reflections on how scholars refer to the acquisition of scientific knowledge as the "Golden Age." Recently, various groups, and even some leaders, in the Arab and Muslim world have recently been expressing in their speeches a nostalgia for that era of enlightenment. Muslim scholars have indeed contributed to the progress of the western medical and scientific advancements of the twenty-first century. Those advancements are based on ideas and methods discovered and pioneered by Muslim scholars such as Al-Khwarizmi, a Persian mathematician, astronomer, and geographer during the Abbasid Caliphate; Ibn Sina in medicine; Sin Ibn Ali in astronomy; Al-Kindi in psychotherapy; and Khalid Ibn Yazid in chemistry, to name but a few. The spread of this knowledge came from the ability to embrace diversity of thoughts and cultures to create a solid foundation for learning. James Wynbrandt writes,

> The strength of the intellectual awakening of the era was in part due to participation of all cultures within the realm. Inclusiveness was a hallmark of the Golden Age. Christians, Nestorians, Jews, and Zoroastrians, along with their brethren Muslim scholars living across the Islamic world from Spain to Persia added immortal masterpieces to the age's cannon. Yet no matter their provenance, the works of the scientists, mathematicians, scholars, poets, and artists from throughout the empire are all considered to be part of the Arab and Islamic patrimony and therefore hold an important place in Arabian history as well.[39]

Tragically, the seventeenth century witnessed the disintegration of the Muslim Empire into smaller countries. Despite this fragmentation, Mecca and Medina retained their spiritual status in the Muslim world. That is why Saudi Arabia now refers to itself as the country of the two holiest sites in the Islamic faith. Every Muslim, if physically and financially able, should visit these two locations to fulfill religious duties known as the pilgrimage, one of the five pillars of Islam.

Historians agree that, during the eighteenth-century era, Saudi Arabian history took shape. It started with a Muslim religious cleric named Muhammad bin Abdul Wahhab, who advocated for followers to return to Islamic principles and adopt them in their pure form. His call for the return to Islam resulted in his persecution by local religious scholars and leaders, who viewed his teachings as a threat to their power base. In a culture that highly valued tribal loyalty, Abdul Wahhab sought protection in the town of Diriyah, located in the northwestern outskirts of the Saudi capital, Riyadh. Interestingly, none other than Muhammad bin Saud ruled Diriyah. Thus began the cooperation between the two powers that shape Saudi Arabia to this day. The two men united for a common goal that would serve their self-interests. Advocating for the application of pure Islam, Muhammad bin Saud saw a political opportunity when he established the first Saudi state. By 1788, the Saudi state expanded its sphere of influence to the city of Najd. Although the Al-Saud tried to forge ties with many tribes to strengthen its position, Madawi al-Rasheed writes, "The Al-Saud's association with the Aniza [tribe], however, remains suspicious since no historical source suggests that this tribal section played a role in their later expansion in Arabia"[40]

Fast-forward to the early nineteenth century. Saudi Arabia had the entire Arabian Peninsula, including Mecca and Medina, under its rule. Modern-day Saudi Arabia started to evolve at that time. The establishment of the first Saudi state, which gained popular support, raised suspicion of the then-Ottoman Empire, considered the dominant force in the Middle East and North Africa at that time. To ensure no other force in the region gained the power sufficient to challenge its dominance, the Ottoman Empire sent troops with modern artillery, in 1818, to fend off the Saudi forces in the western region. The Ottoman forces leveled the city of

Diriyah, rendering it permanently uninhabitable by ruining the wells and uprooting date palms.[41]

Having enjoyed popular support and success during the first phase of the first Saudi state, the Al-Saud family seemed adamant to regain political control in central Arabia. After the Ottomans' destruction of Diriyah, the Saudi ruler, Turki bin Abdullah Al-Saud, decided to move his capital to Riyadh, located about 20 miles south of Diriyah. That move marked the establishment of the second Saudi state. Historians agree that, during his 11-year tenure, Turki bin Abdullah Al-Saud recaptured all lands lost to the Ottomans. Al-Saud learned from what happened when the Ottomans defeated the Saudi forces, so he took the necessary precautions to address his people's concerns. However, Saudi Arabia's period of peace did not last long. In 1865, the Ottoman Empire sought to expand its sphere of influence into the Arabian Peninsula. During this period, Faisal's son, Abdulrahman, ruled Saudi Arabia and fought the Ottomans. The latter captured parts of the Saudi state. Given his inability to fight while facing a well-equipped army, Abdulrahman bin Faisal sought refuge with the Bedouin tribes located in the vast desert swaths of eastern Saudi Arabia known as the Rub' Al-Khali (Empty Quarter). From there, Abdulrahman, along with his family, traveled to Kuwait, where they stayed until 1902. Interestingly, Abdulrahman's son, Abdulaziz, emerged as a fierce warrior, leader, and defender of Islam.

Many historical accounts consider Abdulaziz the founder of modern-day Saudi Arabia. He *was* able to retake Riyadh from the al-Rashid family, who collaborated with the Ottomans. Along with 40 of his followers, Abdulaziz staged a night march into Riyadh and retook the city garrison, known as the Masmak Fortress.[42] It was that event—the night march—that marked the creation of modern-day Saudi Arabia. Abdulaziz's political ambitions extended beyond the borders of Riyadh. He recaptured Hijaz, Mecca, and Medina in 1924 and 1925 respectively. After those victories, Abdulaziz united the tribes under his leadership. In 1932, the Kingdom of Saudi Arabia was officially born.

Emergence of Modern-day Saudi Arabia

Now one sees how Saudi Arabia evolved from a group of nomadic tribes during the early days of Islam into a kingdom. Today, that kingdom wields global influence, especially by producing oil and setting its price. Indeed, one can reasonably argue that the world recognizes Saudi Arabia for two main things: (1) its Wahhabist ideology and (2) its vast oil reserves. Interestingly, those two elements have made Saudi Arabia what it is today, a nation of contradictions, given to religious extremism, while enjoying massive oil wealth. The combination of religious extremism and oil has created a problem, one that contributes to the confusion surrounding Saudi Arabia today. It is no small change to see how oil money has changed the social fabric of Saudi Arabia. Saudi society once wore its storied history as a raiment that it argued imbued it with religious leadership. Money has now attired Saudi society into something altogether different: the costume of pretense, deception, dark secrets, and corruption. Saudi Arabia's petrodollars have corrupted its core values and are fueling religious extremism. Unfortunately, Saudi Arabia claims that its interpretation of Islam indicates the basic principles of the Islamic religion.

The wealthy Saudi Arabia that now appears today seems lost in the wilderness of global chaos. The world is catching on to what Saudi Arabia's Wahhabist ideology means, especially when that ideology is given power by the riches of oil. The desert kingdom needs to examine its Wahhabist ideology *precisely because* of how the world in general and Muslims in particular perceive it. Questions arise: Is Saudi Arabia's Wahhabist ideology responsible for the spread of extremism? Is Saudi Arabia funding terrorist groups? Does Saudi Arabia control the decision-making process in Washington regarding the Middle East? Answering those questions requires us to delve deeper into the history of the desert kingdom to analyze the specific elements—be they religion, tribalism, social norms, customs, economics, or politics—that have shaped the KSA's political views into what they are today. The world, however, continues to focus on one particular strand of Saudi Arabia's social fabric, its Wahhabist ideology.

Saudi Arabia's distant and recent history has been the subject of many academic books, television programs, presentations, conferences, and video documentaries. The following narrative shall neither unfairly criticize

Saudi Arabia nor minimize its support for the Muslim world, no matter how controversial that support may be. This author seeks to present a well-balanced narrative supported by facts and documentation for those with little or no prior knowledge about this contentious country.

The following provides a better understanding of the forces that have made Saudi Arabia what it is today. Understanding basic historical facts about the KSA allows us to place it within the context of the greater Middle East, a volatile region that has always been, and will remain for the future, a center of gravity for the ultimate dreams of conquerors and peacemakers alike. Given that magnetic semblance, the history of modern-day Saudi Arabia testifies to the challenges western powers continue to endure while trying to understand the complexities and challenges this country presented throughout the twentieth century. Yet, the West came to accept Saudi Arabia as it was/is while tolerating its human rights abuses and atrocities.

The following brief account considers key characteristics that shape and influence Saudi Arabia along its evolving path forward. It is a daunting task to cover all aspects of Saudi Arabia's social fabric. The following is limited to topics like geography, religion, demographics, education, government structure, military development and capabilities, energy, and foreign relations. Those characteristics illustrate how, throughout the twentieth century, modern-day Saudi Arabia has progressed.

Geography of Saudi Arabia

Saudi Arabia is known officially as the Kingdom of Saudi Arabia. Its size makes it the fifth-largest state in Asia and second-largest state in the Arab world after Algeria. The KSA borders Jordan and Iraq to the north, Kuwait to the northeast, Qatar, Bahrain and the United Arab Emirates (UAE) to the east, Oman to the southeast and Yemen to the south. The Gulf of Aqaba separates it from Israel and Egypt. In the region, only Saudi Arabia has direct access to both the Red Sea and the Persian Gulf. Furthermore, most of its terrain consists of arid desert and mountains. Yet, Saudi Arabia's rich oil reserves render it a strategic location that bridges not only different economic zones, but also different cultures.

Three bodies of water touch Saudi Arabia. Its Red Sea coastline stretches about 1,760 kilometers (1,100 miles) while its Arabian Gulf coastline roughly 560 kilometers (350 miles). Saudi Arabia is by far the largest country on the Arabian Peninsula. Its borders range from coastlines to dry lands. To the west, the Gulf of Aqaba and the Red Sea form a coastal border of almost 1,800 kilometers that extends south to Yemen and follows a mountain range for approximately 320 kilometers to the vicinity of Najran. This section of the border with Yemen was demarcated in 1934 and is one of the few clearly defined borders with a neighboring country. The Saudi border running southeast from Najran, however, is still undetermined. The undemarcated border became an issue in the early 1990s, when oil was discovered in the area. Following the discovery, Saudi Arabia objected on Yemen's behalf to commercial exploration by foreign companies. In the summer of 1992, representatives of Saudi Arabia and Yemen met in Geneva to discuss settlement of the border issue.[43]

Geographers observe that the Arabian Desert dominates most of Saudi Arabia's official geography. Semidesert, shrubland, and several mountain ranges and highlands mark the landscape. Geographers consider the area of Rub' al Khali (Empty Quarter) in the southeastern part of Saudi Arabia the world's largest contiguous sand desert. Interestingly, Saudi Arabia is the largest country in the world without a river. However, extensive coastlines on the Persian Gulf and Red Sea provide great advantage on shipping (especially crude oil) through the Persian Gulf and Suez Canal.[44] Some of Saudi Arabia's main cities include Riyadh (considered the high-tech center of modern-day Saudi Arabia), Jeddah, Dammam, Al-Khobar, Dhahran, Qatif, Jubail, and Taif.

The KSA is experiencing tremendous population growth. Recent estimates put the total population of Saudi Arabia well over 31 million, including the 30% of expatriates living there. Riyadh, the capital and the largest city in the KSA, is home to over 7 million people. This accounts for over 22% of the population of the whole country.[45] Further, approximately 9 million nonnationals live in Saudi Arabia legally for work or other purposes. The KSA provides no residence for foreigners.

The government of Saudi Arabia does not take a census to determine religion. However, it is known that the KSA is 100% Muslim. However, estimates suggest that the majority of Muslims in Saudi Arabia are of the

Sunni branch of Islam, at 85% to 90%. The other major Muslim group is the Shi'ites, who comprise the remaining 10% to 15% of the community.[46]

Population distribution has been growing progressively over the years. Caryle Murphy, a public policy scholar with the Wilson Center's Middle East Program, writes,

> Saudi Arabia is passing through a unique demographic period. . . . Approximately 37 percent of the Saudi population is below the age of 14. Those under age 25 account for around 51 percent of the population, and when those under 29 are included, young people amount to two-thirds of the kingdom's population. (In the United States, those 14 years and younger are 20 percent of the population; those 29 and below make up 41 percent.). The country's unprecedented "youth bulge" has not yet crested, which means increasing numbers of job-seekers in coming years. This demographic profile is typical of the Gulf region where around 60 percent of the people are under the age of 30, making it one of the most youthful regions in the world.[47]

Saudi Arabia faces serious challenges in addressing the economic demands and meeting the needs of its growing population given the drop in oil prices. Further, the ongoing discontent of its youth in addition to issues in the Shi'a eastern province of Ash-Sharqiyyah could quickly cause things to take a different turn, leading to major demonstrations that could destabilize the monarchy. Could this scenario be what is fueling terrorist recruitment in the KSA?

Most global-affairs, security, and intelligence analysts, Saudi watchers, business leaders, scholars, and historians agree that the KSA defines itself through (a) its Islamic heritage, (b) its historical status as trade center of the Arabian Peninsula, and (c) its tribal traditions and customs, which reflect the hospitality of Arab culture. A changing world requires Saudi Arabia to adapt to these changes; thus, its traditions and lifestyle somehow have to change as well.

The previous chapter discussed the significance of the KSA's geographical location: trade routes converged in the land that is now Saudi Arabia, bringing caravans and merchants from diverse places. That intersection allowed Saudi Arabia to bridge cultural communication and interaction. The location also secured the KSA's identity as the cradle of Arabism, birthplace of Islam, and the site of two holy mosques in the Islamic faith. No one disputes that Saudi Arabia emerged as the final product of a deep-rooted cultural heritage manifested through the rise of empires and the collapse of civilizations once under the banner of Islam. No doubt, modern-day Saudi Arabia combines the economic trade it experienced, the political turmoil it witnessed, and the Islamic faith it embraced. Saudi Arabia's identity thus reflects all those elements, resulting in its having pride in its national heritage. One easily understands why the government of Saudi Arabia allocates funds to preserve archeological sites and emphasizes the need to preserve its national treasures. Undeniably, the KSA's culture and heritage affirm both its presence throughout the ages and its historical contribution. Equally important, this contribution has transformed and shaped the Kingdom of Saudi Arabia from scattered nomadic tribes to a unified country that, largely through its oil, wields global influence.

Arabic is the official language in Saudi Arabia. Many countries in the Middle East and North Africa (MENA), including Egypt, Sudan, Iraq, United Arab Emirates (UAE), Kuwait, Bahrain, Qatar, Jordan, Palestine, Yemen, Oman, Algeria, Tunisia, Morocco, Libya, Syria, and Lebanon share the same language. One should note that to claim that most countries in MENA speak Arabic refers to the ability to *read* classical Arabic, known also as Modern Standard Arabic (MSA). MSA is the language of the holy Qur'an, the sacred book of Islam. If one does not get an education, it will be challenging to read and understand the Qur'an or any other written text in the Arabic language. Regarding spoken Arabic, each country has its own dialect, and those dialects differ from one country to the next based on cultural and historical factors. Consider the Moroccan dialect, for example, which linguists know to be one of the most difficult to learn.

Arabic is one of the oldest languages in the world. It traces its roots to Sanskrit. The earliest example of Arabic inscription dates back to 512 CE. While the Muslim world accounts for about 1.6 billion people, not all of them consider Arabic their primary language. Today, in fact, only about 290 million people in countries like Egypt, Lebanon, Syria, Iraq, Jordan, Kuwait, the UAE, Saudi Arabia, and Oman consider Arabic their first language.[48] Yet, people spoke Arabic before Islam existed. The expansion of Islam and Islamic culture in the 7th century AD facilitated the spread of the Arabic language. Islam allowed the Arabic language to cross the borders of the Arabian Peninsula, spreading north, east, and west. Today, the Arabic language is one of the world's most widely spoken languages.[49]

As previously mentioned, Saudi Arabia takes pride in its historical role in the Arabian Peninsula. This pride also extends to other areas: poetry, folk music (western music is forbidden) and dance (traditional only). In fact, Saudi Arabia celebrates the annual festival of Jenadriyah National Culture and Heritage. This festival is known for one of Saudi Arabia's national dances, dubbed "Al-Ardha." Al-Ardha is a sword dance based on ancient Bedouin traditions: drummers beat out a rhythm, and a poet chants verses while sword-carrying men dance shoulder to shoulder.[50] President Trump was handed a sword during his visit to Saudi Arabia, in May 2017, to perform the national dance with King Salman.

Poetry is another facet of Saudi Arabia's cultural heritage. Most of the Arab world sees poetry as the highest form of expression and revelatory of the beauty of the Arabic language. Yet, this heritage traces its roots to the nomads and Bedouins, who considered poetry a means through which to preserve history, traditions, and social values. Centuries after its inception, poetry remains popular in the Arab and Muslim world in general and Saudi Arabia in particular. For instance, the KSA holds competitions in not only recitation of the Qur'an but also televised poetry.

Education

The first thing that draws the West's attention about education in Saudi Arabia is not how much money the KSA spends on education. It is not the state-of-the-art universities. Rather, it is how Saudi Arabia segregates education by sex. The education system is divided into three separately administered systems: general education for boys, education for girls, and traditional Islamic education for boys. Similarly, western audiences are taken by how Saudi Arabia provides religious teaching and training to its youth, mainly boys, to become clergymen. Note that the education system in the KSA requires memorizing the Qur'an since a large part of the educational curriculum is devoted to religion. Islamic education therefore seems to be the basis of all knowledge. Students further their Islamic studies at universities such as Imam Muhammad bin Saud Islamic University and the Islamic University of Medina.[51] Perhaps the religious influence explains why Muslim societies like Saudi Arabia vehemently oppose secular education.

Some may perceive the education as outdated because it emphasizes Islam. The Saudi royal family and upper class send their offspring to western universities, mainly in the United States and Great Britain, to pursue secular education. If the KSA wants to pursue its Vision 2030, it should restructure its approach to education by acknowledging that its focus on religious education disadvantages its students. Evidence for this claim is Saudi Arabia's having fallen behind the rest of the world. Saudi Arabia has a shortage of doctors, nurses, engineers but an abundance of religious clerics who move society backward through religious interpretations that have nothing to do with Islam (i.e., abolition of women rights, lack of women education, and so on.) Saudi Arabia needs to make changes in order to move forward with the rest of the world. The changes should include adding subjects such as math and science to its general curriculum.

Without a reformed educational system, the Saudi workforce will continue to degrade, thus compelling Saudi Arabia to depend on foreign workers even more than it does now. Further, without change in the educational system, no *skilled* workforce will exist. An unskilled labor force will certainly hinder the crown prince's Vision 2030. Khadija Mosaad, an American-Saudi Arabian expert on global affairs with a focus on higher education in the Middle East, writes,

> Without taking into account the importance, value and overall social implications of a quality education, it is not feasible to implement meaningful economic, cultural and business reforms. Without an educated and skilled workforce, it will be a tremendous challenge for Vision 2030 to meet its target goals. Because of outdated school

curricula, ineffective teaching methods and low education standards, one aspect of the vision that will require extensive improvements is in the field of education. It is estimated that two-thirds of the Saudi population of 29 million are under the age of 30. For Vision 2030 to succeed, Saudi Arabia must take advantage of the knowledge, skills and expertise that this age group can bring to the table.[52]

Experts thus have ongoing concerns over Saudi Arabia's educational system and schools that pursue a curriculum marked with combustible language intolerant of other religions. Yet, based on my understanding of Islam, it has never advocated hatred toward others faiths, including Judaism and Christianity. To be sure, harsh misinterpretations of Islam are apparent even within the faith itself. For instance, religious textbooks in Saudi Arabia label Shia and Sufis (branches of Islam) who disagree with the Saudi interpretation of Islam as *others*. I have never read or heard that Muslims should not associate with non-Muslims. It is nonsense!

My duty is to inform readers about the disparity that exists between what Islam says about *others* versus what Saudi Arabia says about non-Muslims. History shows many examples of non-Muslims living under Muslim rule in which the rights of non-Muslims, freedom of religion, for example, were both guaranteed and protected. Abu Amina Elias writes, "Islam guarantees the protection of Jews, Christians, and other non-Muslims who reside in Muslim lands. Their houses of worship should be defended from attack and their right to worship according to their choice respected. The right to self-defense was granted in Islam in order to protect freedom of religion."[53] These concerns over Saudi Arabia's education system are not new. The question is whether the West has the political will to have an honest debate with the Saudis that goes beyond handshakes and diplomatic niceties. Unfortunately, the United States applies a double standard when addressing this issue with the Saudis: "The United States Department of State first designated Saudi Arabia a 'country of particular concern' under the International Religious Freedom Act for particularly severe violations in 2004. It has continued to do so every year since. The designation should trigger penalties, including economic sanctions, arms embargoes, and travel and visa restrictions. But the US government has had a waiver on penalties in place since 2006. The waiver allows the US to continue economic and security cooperation with Saudi Arabia unencumbered."[54]

In summary, Saudi Arabia must build a skilled, educated workforce to compete in the global economy. If Saudi Arabia wants to succeed in implementing its Vision 2030, it must embark on serious economic programs, emphasize and encourage the exploration of other scientific fields, and refrain from blaming its social ills and extremism on the West. Religion, Islam, in this case, has always advocated for exploring science and knowledge. Harun Yahya writes, "For a sincere Muslim, science is a blessing that God has bestowed on mankind. Islam advocates a rational approach. In many verses of the Quran, God advises people to use their intelligence. He emphasizes the need for us to think rationally and scientifically, speaking of, '...those deeply rooted in knowledge...' and '... only people of intelligence pay heed.' (3:7). Another verse advises people to think about the formation of the universe: '...reflect on the creation of the heavens and the earth...' (3:191)[55] However, if the Kingdom of Saudi Arabia sticks to its puritanical interpretations of Islam and continues to fund its extremist Wahhabist ideology at the calculated exclusion of hard sciences, it will be only a matter of time before demonstrations in the streets of Riyadh, Dammam, Jeddah, Khobar, and Qatif follow. It will be too late by then for Saudi Arabia to save itself.

Structure of the Saudi Government

Saudi Arabia is an absolute monarchy. The king holds the ultimate authority since no written constitution exists. Thus, no checks and balances can challenge the Saudi sovereign's authority. Many called for political reform, in 1992, during the reign of King Fahd. But those calls accomplished nothing. Periodically, since 1962, Saudi kings have promised to establish a *majlis ash shura* (consultative council) to advise them on governmental matters, but none of them took practical steps to establish such a body. The royal family, Al-Saud, simply dominates the government by appointing royal family members to sensitive key positions in the ministries of defense, interior, foreign affairs, and security services. Consequently, the king alone decides the course of action to take on any issue that arises.

The religious establishment guides the political and social course while shaping outcomes, albeit mainly domestic ones. The religious scholar of the KSA is known also as Mufti. The Mufti is chosen and appointed by the king. Given the king's absolute power, it is a forgone conclusion that the Mufti will refrain from criticizing or, in any way, challenging the king's authority, no matter the circumstances. The Mufti issues a religious warning called a *fatwa* that supports the king's agenda; through the *fatwa*, the Mufti holds greater influence on the kingdom's internal affairs.

To maintain total control over the monarchy, the Al-Saud family ensures that the succession to kingship is granted to the sons of the founder, Ibn Saud (King Abdulaziz), and their descendants. Tradition holds that the succession to kingship goes from one brother to the next. The current king, Salman, broke from that tradition by elevating his son, Mohammed Bin Salman (MbS), to crown prince, next in line to the throne. Interestingly, article 5 of the kingdom's Basic Law of Governance, though not a constitutional document, clarifies how the Al-Saud family keeps its firm grip on power. The document reads,

> According to Article 5 of the Basic Law of Governance, rulers of Saudi Arabia will be chosen from amongst the sons of the founder, Ibn Saud (King Abdulaziz), and their descendants. The order of succession to the throne follows agnatic seniority. Since 2006, the Allegiance Council (Hayat al-Baya), consisting of the surviving sons of founder King Ibn Saud, his grandsons whose fathers are deceased, incapacitated, or unwilling to assume the throne, and the sons of the king, decide on the succession to the throne. The King carries the title of the Custodian of the Two Holy Mosques (Khadim al-Haramain al-Sharifain) in Mecca and Medina, which emphasizes the status of Saudi Arabia in the Islamic world.[56]

Given the law, the Saudi royal family should maintain power and drain the kingdom's resources for decades to come. Ironically, it is an open question whether Islam advocates for the existence of a kingdom since Prophet Muhammed *was not* a king; thorough consideration of that question is for another book. Regardless, the Middle East geopolitical landscape is changing, oil prices are dropping, unemployment in Saudi Arabia is rising, and the Wahhabist ideology is under global scrutiny. Saudi Arabia will have to make difficult decisions not only to meet the demands of most of its growing young population, but also to ensure its own survival. Events in the Middle East suggest that KSA is headed in the wrong direction. The recent arrests of scholars and moderate religious leaders in Saudi Arabia raise serious concerns and could serve as a warning of what lies ahead.

Saudi Military Development and Capabilities

If it were not for the support of the United States, Saudi Arabia's military would be unable to defend itself against groups like ISIS, let alone a well-organized military such as that of Turkey, Iran, or pre-2003 Iraq. American support for the KSA is preventing Saudi Arabia from being divided into smaller countries.

Before addressing Saudi Arabia's military capabilities, I discuss KSA's past military structure rather than its strength, since it is far weaker than Iran's, Turkey's, or Iraq during Saddam Hussein's era. The following historical consideration presents a clear picture of the elements that support Saudi Arabia's acquisition and maintenance of its military capabilities. Changing regional politics are forcing Saudi Arabia to strengthen its ties with its allies in the West, mainly Great Britain and the United States. Addressing the scope and kinds of weaponry Saudi Arabia has been purchasing from the West would make an excellent topic of another book. However, my focus in this section is to indicate the origin of those capabilities and explain why KSA is adamant about purchasing the latest, and most expensive, armaments from the West.

It is no secret that the United States and Great Britain are the main weapon suppliers to Saudi Arabia. Yet, China, Russia, Germany, and

France also sell weapons to the KSA. In fact, the last decade has seen steadily increasing weapons exports from EU members, mainly from Germany, France, and the UK to Saudi Arabia. Alix Culbertson writes,

> Arms exports from the EU to both the Middle East and North Africa have significantly increased over the past decade, analysis by the European Union Institute for Security Studies (ISS) found. From 2012 to 2016 the transfer of weapons and military equipment between countries reached its highest volume for any five-year period since the end of the cold war, data from respected think tank the Stockholm International Peace Research Institute (SIPRI) found. Saudi Arabia has seen some of the biggest growth, importing 144 per cent more arms from the EU since 2012 than it did in the five years preceding that.[57]

The most salient questions to ask are why is Saudi Arabia amassing this massive stock of weapons? Is it for regional or international prestige? Is it because the KSA has surplus funds and no other priorities? As a bulwark against Israel? Something fun for the prince to do to alleviate his boredom? Another manifestation of his lavish lifestyle? Or could it be a nice pick-me-up for a defense industry that is about to take a hit as China's and Russia' weapons sales are growing? Turkey's and Iran's recent purchases of Russia's advanced defense missiles, S400 and S300 respectively, show evidence of the preceding claim. Interestingly, in Yemen, Saudi Arabia now uses some of the weapons it bought from the United States. The use put to those weapons raises moral questions that demand answers. Ryan Riegg writes, "While the quantity and purpose of the arms that the Saudis were buying across the world remains something of a mystery, it was not a mystery to the U.S. Shortly after I arrived in Riyadh, President Barack Obama approved a record-breaking $60 billion arms sale to Saudi for weapons that are primarily being used today by the Saudis to bomb Yemen, despite bipartisan objections from the U.S."[58] That report comes on the heels of mounting civilian causalities in Yemen from American and British weapons used by the Saudis. Washington's silence over the atrocities committed in Yemen reflects a failed moral obligation—Washington's surrender to greed, for monetary gain.

Further, declining oil prices on the global market have a tremendous economic impact on Saudi Arabia even as it tries to mask the impact. Yet, the Saudis argue that the massive purchase of weapons is to defend itself from both foreign and domestic threats. Saudi Arabia is an absolute monarchy that prohibits freedom of the press, expression, gathering, and so forth. Who is to say, if demonstrations against the Al-Saud ruling family erupt, that the Saudi government will not use those weapons to quell demonstrations? Adhering to international law is the least of Saudi Arabia's worries as its actions in Yemen demonstrate.

Another school of thought suggests that Saudi Arabia's massive weapons purchases are made to ready itself should another conflict erupt in the Middle East. One possible conflict is a war against Iran—which I do not foresee. The United States may not be in a position to intervene given its past performances in Afghanistan and Iraq. Further, the American people will not support another US engagement in a volatile region of the Middle East. Thus, the Saudis figure that it is in their best interest, and for their survival, to stock up on advanced weapons in case it has to defend itself against domestic or foreign enemies.

A link exists between Saudi Arabia's purchase of weapons and the current economic outlook. The KSA is realizing that oil prices are unlikely to return to their pre-2014 prices of over $100 a barrel. Further, the Saudi economic outlook is grim given that its survival depends mainly on oil revenues. Add to the mix the possibility of the offering of Aramco shares, about 5%, to China,[59] the challenges its Vision 2030 reforms face, and OPEC's production cuts that have failed to live up to expectations now that sanctions against Iran have been lifted and the market is flooded with more oil from Iran.

Another theory explains why the Saudis keep purchasing weapons, especially from the United States. That theory presupposes the Saudis' conviction that the United States will not object to where and how Saudi Arabia deploys those weapons and uses them. In Yemen, for example, Saudi Arabia is still engaged in a three-year-old military intervention that shows no sign of abating. The Saudis' ill-conceived military intervention is causing massive destruction, famine, and humanitarian catastrophe as the KSA continues its barbaric attacks with impunity. What happened to America's moral leadership? Why are American leaders—and the West, for that matter—not standing up against the atrocities Saudi Arabia is committing against defenseless Yemenis using western/American weapons? As one who spent time in Yemen supporting US foreign-policy initiatives, I witnessed the poverty, lack of infrastructure, and tremendous struggle for average Yemenis to make ends meet. It was heart breaking. Given President Trump's recent visit to Saudi Arabia and his seemingly isolationist foreign policy, it is my opinion that Saudi Arabia may have interpreted that as doing whatever it wants since its patron, the US, would not object. What has become of America? I continue to wonder. Ryan Riegg writes, "That the U.S. political elite lack backbone. For the past several years, the Saudis have funneled guns and weapons to ISIS and bombed the near-defenseless country of Yemen with impunity. Therefore, the Saudis may believe that they can do whatever they want and the U.S. will not react, especially given Barack Obama's failure to enforce his 'red line' in Syria and speeches by Donald Trump indicating an isolationist worldview that would keep the U.S. out of the Middle East."[60]

Another argument suggests that Saudi Arabia wants to position itself militarily in case its interests collide with Iran's. Iran's expanding influence and increasing military capabilities lend support to that claim. Indeed, many defense analysts suggest that Iran's military capabilities outmatch those of Saudi Arabia, especially its naval capability and missile accuracy. The latter assertion compels me to address Saudi Arabia's missile force. Saudi Arabia's missile technology is outdated and weak in comparison to that of Iran, Israel, and Turkey. The southern missile base the KSA kept secret for some time is now exposed; there is, however, nothing of great importance about that missile site. The site, Al-Sulayyil, is the first Saudi ballistic missile facility, built in 1987 or 1988 near the town of Al-Sulayyil, 450 kilometers southwest of the Saudi Arabian capital, Riyadh. It houses Dong Feng-3, Chinese missiles known for their poor accuracy, according to commercial satellite imagery.

Fast-forward to 2014. Things have changed dramatically. Saudi Arabia made it publicly known, through a parade, that it now has missile launchers. Its government-approved social media even posted some images online of the DF3. Note that another type of Chinese missile, the DF-21, is far more accurate than the DF3. Jeffery Lewis, director of the East Asia Nonproliferation Program for the James Martin Center for Nonproliferation Studies at the Middlebury Institute of International Studies at Monterey, writes, "It used to be that Saudi Arabia did not want to call attention to its budding missile force. Khalid shrouded his '80s trip to China, and the ensuing shipments, in secrecy. Although news of the sale eventually broke, and although information about Saudi Arabia's new missile bases near Sulayyil and Jufayr appeared in the press, Saudi officials kept mum."[61]

Despite Saudi Arabia's clandestine purchase of the Chinese missile technology, many analysts argue that the KSA, and other Gulf states, still prefer US weapons—and, to a lesser extent, British and French hardware—due to their accuracy and effectiveness:

> In addition to military training, U.S. defense relations are underpinned by huge defense equipment deals. U.S. military hardware (and, to a lesser extent, British and French hardware) is preferred across the region because of its effectiveness and symbolic value as a sign of a close security relationship, and much of it has been combat tested. For example, Kuwait, the UAE, Jordan, and Saudi Arabia have over 400 F-15, F-16, and F/A-18 jet fighter aircraft combined. Following the Iran nuclear deal, threatened Arab states undertook military buildups and a flood of arms purchases. The U.S. approved $33 billion worth of weapons sales to its Gulf Cooperation Council allies between May 2015 and March 2016.[62]

I still wonder whether the purchase of weapons will save Saudi Arabia in the not-so-distant future should it face a domestic revolt or demonstrations of unprecedented intensity. Both could happen given the high unemployment, discrimination against minorities (Shi'ites), and increasing poverty (widening gap between poor and rich). Saudi Arabia will eventually wake up to the reality that money can go only so far in solving problems.

Saudi Arabia's Foreign-Policy Structure

Here is how the story goes: Saudi Arabia is destined to play a leadership role in the foreign policy of the volatile Middle East. However, reality suggests that it has no such role. Saudi Arabia is playing a leadership role? Are we kidding ourselves? It must have been a dream to expect the KSA to fill the vacuum left by the United States' declining leadership in the region. How could it when the KSA's foreign policy is chaotic, unsound, and fallacious? One must have been generous even to use the term "foreign policy" regarding Saudi Arabia. In my opinion, the only two elements that define the KSA's version of foreign policy are oil and Wahhabism. Allow me to explain. The discovery of oil in the 1930s allowed the KSA to inject itself into the global economy. It was not because of a set of effective policies or creative ideas. Rather, it was because the world was moving toward a global market that demanded access to energy resources. Saudi Arabia's vast unexplored oil fields positioned it to meet those demands. Thus, US-Saudi relations were born. The deal is as it has been from the inception of relations. Saudi Arabia provides oil to the United States at a cheaper price in return for security. That's it—it's enough to make one's head spin, trying to extrapolate any kind of cohesive policy from that arrangement! The second part of Saudi Arabia's so-called foreign policy comes from its exporting Wahhabism, its puritanical, twisted, and intolerant version of Islam. Interestingly, this version of Islam is *not* practiced anywhere in the Muslim world except in Saudi Arabia and limited areas in Pakistan, Afghanistan, Bangladesh, Kosovo, Nigeria, Philippines, Indonesia, and Sudan. Wahhabism has established a foothold in those countries.

However, we cannot address Saudi Arabia's foreign policy without bringing into the conversation the close ties this ultraconservative monarchy has with the United States. Is it fair to say that US-Saudi relations are of strategic convenience? Most analyses point in that direction. A plethora of national, regional, and global shared interests ensures the survivability of this relationship for decades to come. I go even further: when the inevitable demise of Al-Saud becomes clear to Washington, US policymakers will intervene to save the monarchy because there so much is at stake. Fahad

Nazer, a nonresident fellow at the Arab Gulf states Institute in Washington, writes:

> What some have called the "Salman doctrine" appears predicated on the idea that the unprecedented tumult that has gripped the region requires Saudi Arabia to play a leadership role. It holds that the Saudis must fill the vacuum left by the United States by adopting an assertive foreign policy to bring a modicum of stability to the region, one that is not averse to the use of force when necessary. While political differences between the two governments should not be dismissed, bilateral relations between the two countries have not endured for over seven decades by happenstance. A plethora of mutual interests will ensure that Saudi Arabia and the United States will remain important allies for the foreseeable future. This is especially the case in the old "oil-for-security" equation, which had sustained the relationship for decades. It has been reformulated in light of the shale oil revolution in the United States that made it less dependent on oil imports and as the Saudi armed forces' military capabilities have improved significantly in recent years.[63]

A consensus among scholars, intelligence analysts, and global-affairs experts is that Saudi Arabia's foreign policy is marked by (a) inconsistencies and (b) controversies. The inconsistencies manifest themselves in proxy wars against other Muslim countries. Saudi Arabia's ongoing failed military intervention in Yemen is one example. The controversies result from Saudi Arabia's exportation of its Wahhabist ideology, which places the KSA under global scrutiny, especially with the rise of the likes of Al-Qaeda, ISIS, and other jihadist groups. Current conversations among international security analysts echo serious concerns over the expansion of Saudi Wahhabism beyond Pakistan, Afghanistan, Nigeria, and Sudan. More recently, the ideology has begun to conquer Europe. From my perspective, the KSA exports Wahhabism as a foreign-policy tool to demonstrate its ability to manipulate Muslims about Islam. Such manipulation serves the desert kingdom's interests by rallying the masses under the banner of Islamic unity. Yet, one can understand the complexity and ambiguity of Saudi foreign policy, as F. Gregory Gause III argues, in terms of two main objectives: (1) to protect the country from any foreign invasion, and (2) to ensure the stability, survival, and domination of the Al-Saud regime for millennia to come.[64]

Chapter 3 details why and how Saudi Arabia structures, implements, and executes its foreign policy. Saudi Arabia's approach demonstrates the two edges of the Wahhabist sword. On the one hand, the propagation of the Wahhabism ideology serves Saudi Arabia as self-promotion of leadership in the Muslim world, a role most of the Muslim world neither agrees with nor appreciates. On the other hand, recall that Muhammed Abd Wahhab, the founder of Wahhabism, joined forces with the first Saudi ruler, Abdulaziz, to establish Saudi Arabia. I argue that the Al-Saud could not turn their backs on the religious establishment that provided them with much-needed religious legitimacy. Where is the connection between the two, one may ask? The answer lies in that, over the years, exporting Wahhabism, an extreme version of Islam that has nothing to with the teaching of the religion, became an essential tool in the KSA's foreign-policy toolbox directed under the close supervision of the Al-Saud family.[65] Because of this approach to foreign policy, Saudi Arabia remains a controversial country and an irrational state. The world comes to see Saudi Arabia as the source of terrorism in spite of the desert kingdom's rhetoric to the contrary.

Viewing Saudi Arabia as the source of terrorism? How could that not be when the Saudi leadership refused to condemn the message Wahhabism is propagating by issuing dress codes, forcing men to wear foot-long beard, and denying girls the right to an education. This guidance created the likes of Osama Bin Laden, Mullah Omar, Al-Zarqawi and, more recently, Abu Bakr Al-Baghdadi. Bin Laden's message was both conceived and taught in the schools and madrassas within Saudi Arabia. Bin Laden's death, in May 2011, will not end terrorism against the United States as long as the teaching of the Wahhabist ideology in the madrasas' curriculum in Saudi Arabia persists. People like Bin Laden will return in the future. The argument is to what degree Wahhabism serves Saudi Arabia's interests, be they religious, social, or ideological. David Ottaway writes, "Wahhabism provides the kingdom with its distinct character, and its religious precepts act as a very powerful glue holding the country's myriad tribes together."[66]

Saudi Arabia's leadership is unwilling to enact reforms that allow it to play an effective leadership role on the global stage and the Muslim world. Robert Bear, a former CIA operative, echoed this sentiment in his book *Sleeping with the Devil*. He argues that the United States' government has failed to make it clear to Riyadh that the funding of terrorism has to stop, and dependence on Saudi oil must cease. Otherwise, Saudi Arabia's extremist ideology will continue to hold the US hostage precisely because of US addiction to oil. Extremely vulnerable to economic disaster, the United States will be at risk for acts of terrorism beyond those of the 9/11 attacks.[67]

Religion

Is it fair to say that Islam and oil are the only possibilities that Saudi Arabia has at its disposal when transacting with the world? Absolutely! Even more intriguing and concerning, at the same time, is that the version of Islam Saudi Arabia promotes is utterly incorrect, misguided, dangerous, and contrary to the true teachings of Islam. As one who was born in the culture, is well acquainted with the Arab and Islamic tradition, speaks its language, and understands its social interactions and dynamics, I can attest that the twisted interpretations of Islam sponsored through Wahhabism have nothing to do with Islam. Saudi Arabia's purpose in promoting this intolerable, twisted version of Islam plays a pivotal role in framing the debate over two key elements on which the KSA's foreign policy is based: petrodollars and Wahhabism.

My focus herein is on how the expansion of Islam in Saudi Arabia, home to the two holiest sites, Mecca and Medina, allows the KSA to claim a de facto leadership role over the Muslim world—a role many Muslim countries do not recognize. Let me explain in the following snapshot how Islam started.

The prophet Muhammed was born in Mecca (ca. 570-632). Muslims believe that Muhammed received the revelations from God through the angel Gabriel. Over time, those revelations were collected and codified into what is known as the "Noble Qur'an." Muslims believe that the Qur'an revelations are God's words on events that happened during the prophet's era. Similarly, the Qur'an provides guidelines for how one should conduct his or her life and be responsible for his or her own actions. Moreover, God *alone* will be the final judge, not some self-appointed imam, a religious establishment appointed by a royal degree, or a sitting president. What upsets Muslims—at least the younger generation—around the world is when they, for instance, hear that the Saudi religious establishment has the ultimate authority to decide on this issue or that issue. A few examples follow: a woman must walk some five feet behind the man; a woman's place is at home, not in a professional setting; education is mainly for males but not females; and a woman has to cover from head to toe. This is clearly Saudi Wahhabist ideology spreading extreme ideas while attaching the word *Islam* to its twisted interpretations, thus legitimizing these statements with religious authority. Nonsense, I argue! Take, for instance, the wearing of the "Abaya," which covers women from head to toe. How many times have we heard that it is a traditional Islamic dress code for women? I can confirm that the dress is completely *un-Islamic*, as the Qur'an or Sunna (the verbally transmitted record of teachings, deeds, and sayings of the prophet Muhammad) neither require nor prescribe it. Rather, the Abaya is a tribal tradition limited to pockets of the Muslim world, including Afghanistan, Saudi Arabia, Kuwait, Iran, Yemen, Pakistan, and other countries.

Throughout the history of humanity, whether Judaism, Christianity, or Islam, religion has advanced specific agendas. Islam is no different in this context. When Saudi Arabia promotes its agenda by wrapping it in a religious narrative, it uses Islam to rally the masses, the majority of whom are uneducated, forcing acceptance of Riyadh's cultural norms. Does the reader recall when Saudi Arabia supported the Taliban in Afghanistan? Does the reader realize how many petrodollars Saudi Arabia allocated to building madrassas in Pakistan, Sudan, and Indonesia to promote its Wahhabist ideology? Examples abound! Leaders not only in Saudi Arabia but also in other Muslim countries must fully understand the power of religion in politics. When they want to push or justify their agenda, all they have to do is use the word "Islam," and the masses will submit because they will not question the leader's argument since Islam forbids it. Most Muslims are conditioned not to challenge religion but to accept it as presented. I believe that unquestioning acceptance is where the problem lies within the Muslim world.

To illustrate, the pilgrimage to Mecca, one of the five pillars of Islam, obligates Muslims to perform it if they are financially and physically able. That means Muslims must travel to Saudi Arabia, where the two holy sites of Mecca and Medina are located. The pilgrimage requires Muslims to conduct a series of rituals to meet the religious requirements associated with the journey. Yet, since Mecca and Medina are located in Saudi Arabia, the latter takes it upon itself to politicize the pilgrimage as it sees fit, sometimes using it to punish pilgrims from a specific Muslim country for disagreeing with the kingdom's policies. For instance, last year, Saudi Arabia barred Iranian pilgrims from attending the Hajj (pilgrimage.)[68] This year, it was Qatar's turn to be barred due to ongoing tensions between Saudi Arabia and Qatar. The latter's National Human Rights Committee (NHRC) filed a complaint with the United Nations special rapporteur on freedom of belief and religion over access to Mecca and Medina.[69] Who knows which Muslim country will next be subject to the ban? These series of events clearly demonstrate how Saudi Arabia uses religion for punishment when doing so is wrong. From a religious perspective, visiting Mecca and Medina as part a pilgrimage *should not* and *must not* be politicized and subject to political reprisals. It is a violation of faith. I believe Muslims should boycott going on the pilgrimage all together. God, after all, knows what is in one's heart, and His mercy and grace, *not* prayers and devotion, earn one access to His paradise.

A Westerner finds it challenging to understand Saudi Arabia's contradictory policies and the propagation of its Wahhabist ideology. Thus, we should be humble and honest in admitting our limitations and inabilities to fathom what and how the KSA structures its foreign policy using Islam as its main tool. As I argued in *Volatile State: Iran in the Nuclear Age*, western audiences are presented with inaccurate accounts of Iran, for instance. For example, it has been poorly explained to people in the West that Persia and Iran are the same country. Further, western media presents a different picture of Iran, one of deep contradictions within the country. I have argued before that even American visitors to Iran disagree with the western media's negative portrayal of Iran.[70] Saudi Arabia is no different. It is challenging for outsiders to understand the fears and strategies that guide and drive the desert kingdom to (a) use the Wahhabist ideology (masked under the banner of Islam), (b) fund terrorism (Al-Qaeda and the likes), and (c) build madrassas in different corners of the Muslim world (Pakistan, Afghanistan, Sudan, and others) as tools in its foreign-policy toolbox. Doing so requires access to the highest level of government, which is impossible. Interestingly, in Kenneth Pollack's article, "Fear and Loathing in Saudi Arabia," Greg Gause said it best of Saudi Arabia's politics: "those who know don't speak, and those who speak don't know."[71]

Conclusion

Subsequent pages provide a detailed narrative of Saudi Arabia's justification for deploying religion to support its domestic and global agenda. The time could not be more challenging and puzzling for the KSA as the Middle East spirals out of control, oil prices drop, Iran's influence grows, and President Trump makes one of his biggest foreign-policy blunders, thus far, by decertifying the Iran nuclear agreement. The KSA's fears are also internal: growing unemployment, a widening gap between the rich and the poor, and systemic inequalities. The list is long.

Chapter 3 focuses on which sources Saudi Arabia draws its power from to support its domestic and global agenda. Yet, the KSA's main foreign-policy priority aims to counter anything that threatens the survival of the Al-Saud dynasty. The complicated, multilevel security threats and geopolitical dynamics in the Middle East make it even more challenging for Saudi Arabia to know for sure the strategy to pursue to address those challenges. Furthermore, oil prices are a major source of revenue. Those revenues support the Al-Saud family's lavish lifestyle, albeit one that goes against the teaching of Islam. Falling oil prices compel the Saudi leaders to forge ventures with Russia and China, a pivot that would be unthinkable in the not-too-distant past.

Make no mistake: the choices Saudi Arabia has to make, eventually, regarding competing foreign-policy goals will prove a significant challenge. The KSA has never had to face an existential dilemma since, in the last 70 years, the United States covered it under its security umbrella. Interesting times lie ahead for Saudi Arabia!

CHAPTER III

Saudi Arabia's Sources of Power

Introduction

Debates that began in 2011 continue today. The question is whether Saudi Arabia can handle the violent mess in the Middle East. Business leaders and political observers in addition to defense, intelligence, and energy analysts are speculating about the stability of the desert kingdom. Their concerns started soon after the Arab Spring demonstrations in 2011 that created pockets of protests in North Africa and the Middle East (MENA) region. Now that the newly appointed crown prince, Mohammed bin Salman (MbS), is next in line to the throne, how will he handle force-producing challenges (the Syrian civil war, Yemen's quagmire, Iran's growing influence, and Russia and China's increasing footprints in the region)? MbS lacks foreign-policy experience and still has much to learn about managing global relations and domestic affairs.

The question whether Saudi Arabia can maintain its stability presupposes antecedent questions: What is the source of Saudi Arabia's power? If those sources of power are religion and oil, are there others besides? Grant the previous chapters' arguments that Saudi Arabia draws its power from religion and oil. Now, my analysis focuses on whether those sources continue to provide the KSA an opportunity for Saudi Arabia to play an influential role in a fast-changing world. This chapter offers a detailed narrative that addresses those basic questions.

The complexities of current political, ethnic, social, and economic conditions in the Middle East cast doubt on Saudi Arabia's ability to address, let alone influence, the outcome in its favor. The Yemen quagmire, planned and executed by the inexperienced crown prince, MbS, exemplifies the problem. That flashpoint provides one with a glimpse into the chaotic initiatives and myopic vision of the Saudi foreign-policy establishment.

While on the subject of MbS, one must point out that the decision by King Salman to elevate his son, MbS, to crown prince suggests an internal power struggle already in the making. Further, this elevation of MbS contradicts the hierarchy of the Saudi royal family, in place since its inception. I strongly believe that MbS faces serious challenges once he becomes king, challenges that go beyond his inexperience, reckless policies, and impulsiveness. In my opinion, those challenges could directly affect both Saudi Arabia's stability and the monarchy's survival.[72]

The Middle East was and is the most volatile region in the world; it will continue to be the epicenter of military, sectarian, and social conflicts for the near future. It will also continue to be a competitive arena for global powers to exert their influence and profit from its bountiful economic resources. One realizes the volatility of the region when President Trump, for instance, decertified the Iran nuclear agreement. Mr. Trump's decision certainly changes the geopolitical calculus for not only Iran, but also other regional countries, including Saudi Arabia. I argue that the decision to decertify the Iran nuclear agreement is already playing into the hands of Iran's hardliners. By contrast, the decertification of the deal is music to the ears of the Saudis. Besides Saudi Arabia, the United Arab Emirates (UAE) and Israel ███████████████████████████ are the only countries to welcome this step by the American president. Most other countries disagree with Trump's decision. Stephen Castle of the *New York Times* writes, "Though they avoided direct criticism of Mr. Trump, Prime Minister Theresa May of Britain, Chancellor Angela Merkel of Germany and President Emmanuel Macron of France said in rare joint statement that they 'stand committed' to the 2015 Nuclear Deal and that preserving it was 'in our shared national security interest.'"[73] Notably, Russia and China have already expressed dismay at the Trump administration's decision. Other disturbing events accompany the rejection of the Iran nuclear deal. Consider, for example, Iraqi forces' takeover and direct control of the strategic oil-rich city of Kirkuk from Kurdistani authority. Witness the failed states of Yemen and Libya, the ongoing civil war in Syria, and security and political chaos in Egypt. I wonder whether Saudi Arabia is in position, for instance, to balance its foreign-policy objectives while addressing the ongoing upheavals.

One thing is for certain: If it had no massive oil wealth, Saudi Arabia would have been lost in the dust of history. Perhaps it would have been divided into small countries. However, the presence of an overabundance of oil gives Saudi rulers potentially unlimited influence—financial and economic, at least. Those resources need to be used discreetly. Massive oil wealth has allowed Saudi leaders, past and present, to purchase stability at home, export and spread the Wahhabist ideology in the Middle East and beyond, and subdue governments who disagree with its policies, whatever they may be.

Now let us consider the sources of Saudi Arabia's power more closely, specifically, religion and oil. In my opinion, religion and oil primarily contribute to how the Kingdom of Saudi Arabia structures its foreign policy and serves its interests domestically and globally. However, it perplexes me to read professors Isam Yahia Al Filali of King Abdulaziz University in Jeddah, Saudi Arabia, and Giulio Gallarotti, Wesleyan University, Middletown, Connecticut, USA, arguing otherwise. Consider this statement from a paper they coauthored, in 2013: "Historically, a principal and the most consistent source of Saudi power at the domestic, regional and global levels has not been revenues from oil, but the cultural power that inheres in a Kingdom that is both the capitol of the Muslim and Arab worlds."[74] While the professors may have based their argument on a particular aspect at a particular time, I respectfully disagree with their assessment given how Saudi Arabia has been perceived around the world, at least since 9/11. So, let us delve deeper into why and how Saudi Arabia draws its power from religion.

Islam: A Source of Power

In Saudi Arabia's case, the Al-Saud ruling family uses Islam as a set of unifying cultural symbols, for political legitimization, and for social control. Significant here is the Al-Saud ruling family's alliance with 'Ulama, the religious establishment. The Al-Saud family gives 'Ulama command of the legal system, and, in return, it sanctions the Al-Saud's dynastic rule. In Saudi Arabia, the ruling family's usage of Islam, however, has become a two-edged sword. Using Islam to that end could also lead to criticisms of the ruling elite and calls for governmental policy change. On the other hand, the neopatrimonial approach focuses on the consequences of eventual contradictions between traditional structures of authority and the logic of the modern, state-centered conception of authority. Saudi Arabia clearly fits into Max Weber's definition of a neopatrimonial state. Its staff and administrative units are fairly advanced, but, in terms of its ethos, it presupposes the absolute rule of the Al-Saud and the favoritism it enjoys from the royalty.

Saudi Arabia argues that it is the only Muslim country in the world worthy to carry the banner of Islam. Two facts support its claim: Islam originated there, and Saudi Arabia contains within its territory the two holiest sites in Islam, Mecca and Medina. I agree that Mecca and Medina are located in Saudi Arabia. However, it perplexes me how having two of Islam's holy sites grants a country the right to claim leadership within the Islamic world. Is the right given through a divine promise that no one knows about? More likely, the aim of this claimed leadership is to influence the policies and outcomes of various domestic and foreign agendas. In that case, I can certainly understand Saudi Arabia's logic for claiming leadership over the Muslim world. How convenient it is for Saudi Arabia to use Islam as a source of power!

Saudi watchers, business leaders, and intelligence and global-affairs analysts continue to wonder how long this power may last. Under their forms of influence, the Al-Saud has undoubtedly enjoyed a long, continuous domestic stability. However, current political, social, and economic dynamics in the Middle East are changing rapidly. Moreover, the desert kingdom is finding it hard to keep up with the changes. Amid the current chaos and violent scenarios of the Middle East, besides the KSA's growing tensions with Iran, Saudi Arabia is acting irrationally on two main fronts: militarily (engagement in an unnecessary proxy war in Yemen) and economically (influencing oil production for the sole purpose of punishing Iran economically). Countries that receive low levels of funding from Saudi Arabia's financial spending see Saudi Arabia as a leader. However, others question the rationale on which the KSA bases its strategy in dealing with the region—and the world, for that matter. That said, Saudi Arabia stands to benefit religiously or economically from its leadership, whether by design or by default.

Much has been written on Saudi Arabia as a contradictory, complex country. Those narratives range from its foreign-policymaking process and the export of its Wahhabist ideology, to monetary policies and energy outlook. Little has been concluded in terms of whether Saudi Arabia can sustain its leadership role given the ongoing upheavals in the Middle East, the rising power of Iran, and the security challenges emanating from Syria, Yemen, Libya, and Egypt. We are not compelled to address Saudi Arabia's hard power—it has none. Instead, we can highlight its soft power, especially its soft power *through religion*. Given that Saudi Arabia is home to the two most holy sites in the Islamic faith, Mecca and Medina, this reality allows it to claim religious authority over the Muslim world. The notion that Muslim countries, not only in the Middle East but also throughout the Muslim world, act as a coherent entity is a myth. No goodwill, unity, or harmony exists. The blockade on Qatar and ongoing slaughter in Yemen serve as examples. Simon Mabon writes, "…In addition, it challenges the notion that states within the Middle East are coherent, unitary actors, suggesting instead that in order to fully understand the behaviour of a state, one must consider the importance of internal dynamics. The internal challenges that a state faces, if severe enough, can result in an internal security dilemma, the resolution of which has the capacity to complicate the external security environment."[75]

Bear in mind Mabon's point. It is, then, fair to state that Saudi Arabia remains a country beset by social tensions. Those tensions exist between Islamic authorities who want to preserve a harsh, twisted interpretation of Islam and the youth who want to join the international community while maintaining their Islamic identity. Massive oil wealth merely masks the serious underlying tensions beneath the surface of Saudi society. Once again, I am not writing to criticize Saudi Arabia unfairly. Rather, I am providing the kingdom with an opportunity to see its reflection in the mirror of reality, so the Saudi leadership can plan accordingly. Reflective self-awareness can lead to the formulation of comprehensive domestic and foreign policies that march in lockstep with the current changes experienced by the world. I note that the Saudi royal family worries most about *internal* challenges. Those ideological and social concerns prompt the Al-Saud dynasty to think in terms of deploying its petrodollars and use Islam as a tool not only to claim religious leadership in the Muslim world but also to secure its legitimacy at home. Most Muslims unquestioningly obey Islam, yet they question Christianity and Judaism, which I find hypocritical. It seems to me a forgone conclusion that the Muslim world will let stand the twisted interpretations of Islamic teachings emanating from the Wahhabist establishment in Saudi Arabia. One need only see, for instance, how Saudi Arabia uses the title for the monarch: "King (whomever), Protector of the Two Holy places. The Custodian of the Two Holy Mosques." (Mabon, p. 87).

That title suggests Saudi Arabia's realization that the source of its power, at least within the kingdom and the Muslim world at large, lies not in acquiring territories or building a military power, though it continues to purchase military hardware from the USA and the UK. Rather, it relies on the Wahhabist ideology to push its agenda. Of note, Wahhabism occupies a prominent place in the Saudi society due to its historical ties. The relationship and alliance between the Al-Saud and Wahhabi clerics goes back centuries. Thus, the relevant question is: Does Saudi Arabia draw its power from religion? Absolutely!

With this in mind, one must address why Saudi Arabia uses Islam to further its domestic and foreign policies. Why does it choose Wahhabism rather than, let us say, moderate Islam? Recently, Crown Prince MbS's call for the modernity of Saudi Arabia, cultural exchanges with the West, mainly the USA, and liberation of the kingdom from its twisted religious conservatism raised some eyebrows. I believe those statements by MbS are nothing but flowery speeches and empty promises given that the economic, social, and geopolitical, challenges the KSA faces could devastate the kingdom if addressed incorrectly. I also wonder if the religious establishment within Saudi Arabia will allow such a transformation. As of this writing, a campaign of arrests ordered by the Saudi leadership could easily undermine the efforts Saudi Arabia tries to achieve. "These apparently politically motivated arrests are another sign that Mohammed bin Salman has no real interest in improving his country's record on free speech and the rule of law,"[76] Sarah Leah Whitson, Human Rights Watch's Middle East director, writes.

Let us put that statement within the context of how Saudi Arabia uses religion to control the domestic agenda. Ones does not have to look far to realize how the twisted interpretation of Islam's Wahhabist clerics, funded by the Saudi government, aims at two things: blaming the West for all its social ills and preventing Saudi youths from learning about the world and integrating. In consequence, Saudi youth are forced to accept those interpretations, which, in turn, suppresses any domestic uprising and guarantees the survival and stability of the Al-Saud monarchy. John Bradley, a journalist who worked in Saudi Arabia, writes:

> For seven decades, generation after generation of Saudis has grown up being told at school by Wahhabi-inspired teachers that the West is the source of all evil. At the same time, they have been forced to accept, also without question, that the very survival of the kingdom's ruling elite – and the development of its infrastructure – is entirely dependent on its intimate cooperation with the West. How to reconcile the pride, even arrogance of the former with the at least implicit admission of weakness of the latter? Saudi youth partake in the bounty of the West, are able to buy the latest consumer goods, which exposes them all the more easily to its temptations.[77]

Saudi Arabia draws its power from religion in part because separation between church (or mosque, in this example) and state (government) does not exist in Saudi Arabia or the Islamic faith, for that matter. If a nation fails to adhere to the concept of separation between church and state, any government in the Muslim world can justify whatever policies and agendas it wants to push on the pretext of religious guidelines and the religious duty to follow them. Said differently, Saudi Arabia illustrates how religious clerics sometimes write rules and prohibitions under the religious banner when the Qur'an, or hadith, the collection of the prophet's sayings, has no basis for those rules and prohibitions. The dress a Muslim woman wears, the Burqa—also known as *chadri* or *paranja* in Central Asia—that covers her from head to toe is one example. Thomas Lippman writes, "The best-known example of a Saudi rule that the muttawain enforce without any real religious justification is the prohibition on women driving. Even government officials and senior princes of the royal family have acknowledged it has no basis in Islamic law. No other country enforces such a ban, but in Saudi Arabia the rules of the faith and the force of custom have become so conflated that the senior religious scholars and preachers, known collectively as ulama, or learned ones, have a powerful influence on matters that in other countries would not concern them."[78]

As of September 2017, King Salman issued a royal decree that grants every eligible Saudi woman the right to drive if she wants. The royal decree also suggests that women will need neither permission from a legal guardian to get a driver's license nor a guardian present in the car with her when driving alone.[79] It is important to acknowledge the baby steps that Saudi Arabia is taking to recognize women's basic rights such as driving, in turn allowing Saudi society to join the international community. King Salman's order sends a message to the religious establishment that the time for promoting twisted interpretations of Islam is nearing an end. It states that Wahhabism has to conform or else. The decree suggests that Saudi Arabia wishes to catch up with the world rather than lag behind and recognizes that the Saudi youth deserve a better future. However, the West should not interpret the decree as the willingness, finally, of the conservative KSA to embark on a democratic journey. That is wishful thinking, and I believe it will never happen. Democracy is incompatible with Arab/Muslim systems of governance. I see no compelling reason or evidence that Saudi Arabia will relinquish its control of religion to sustain its worldwide Muslim leadership, which has been acquired by default.

As stated earlier, Muslims learn, at an early age, not to question their religion, or the Qur'an, or clerics, and so forth. Saudi Arabia continues to adopt similar approaches when justifying its position on domestic issues and when dealing with foreign governments. Saudi Arabia uses religion knowing that Islam rules, and the masses submit. Saudi Arabia knows that the fatwa (religious decree) is issued by clerics appointed and funded by the government to provide religious legitimacy. Saudi Arabia knows that studying religion at the calculated exclusion of hard sciences (math, physics, astronomy, et al.) is a duty. In addition, how could religious clerics in Saudi Arabia forbid questioning any religious matters when God allows such questioning? As one familiar with the Holy Qur'an, I point to a verse in chapter 2 (Al-Baqra) in which angels question God for his decision to create Adam and set him up as His deputy on earth: "Are You placing in it (the earth) whom will corrupt it and shed blood, while we celebrate Your praise and sanctify You?"[80] they ask. Interestingly, God does not reprimand the angels for asking. Rather, he replies to them that the wisdom of the matter transcends their comprehension. Therefore, the notion that Muslims cannot question Islam is nonsense! These tactics—which I strongly believe the religious establishment supports and even pushes—trace their roots back to the time of Ahmad Ibn Taymiyah, a thirteenth-century theologian who argued that religious scholars should rank above the ruler as people's moral steward. So, when a government, Saudi or otherwise, finds that the religious establishment offers it the platform from which to control the population, it becomes easy for that government to issue whatever orders it wants while attaching the word "Islam" to those orders to give them religious legitimacy. Doing so provides the government the much-needed power to control other aspects of people's daily lives. The Taliban in Afghanistan, Al-Shabab in Somalia, and Abu Sayyaf in Philippines show how governments distort Islam to carry out their political will. That said, the restrictions the Saudi government—and others, for that matter—place on their citizens under the banner of Islam aim at one thing: absolute power and control.

Religion is a basic tenet of Saudi Arabia's existence, which includes social and intellectual life, since it has no political parties, checks and balances, elections, and so forth. As a result, Islam is the path through which the Al-Saud monarchy controls the country's massive oil wealth and funds its lavish lifestyle to the detriment of an oppressed, deprived society. As a result, the Al-Saud government is compelled to defend the status quo at any cost. Intriguingly, at least from an outsider's perspective, the Al-Saud dynasty decided to legitimize its rule by showing its support for Islam. It sought out its longtime religious ally, the conservative Wahhabist establishment. For this reason alone, Saudi Arabia bestowed upon its king the title of "Khadim al-Haramayn al-sharifayn," which translates into "Custodian of the Two Holy Mosques." Two other variant translations exist for the same title: "Servant of the Two Noble Sanctuaries" and "Protector of the Two Holy Cities." However one translates the title—and, though it has a religious connotation—it ultimately serves a political objective. Granting the king the title automatically legitimizes the political rule of the king and his family. Under those circumstances, one wonders to what degree the rulers of Saudi Arabia use Islam to justify their firm grip on power. Yet, the title has proven to be a two-edged sword. On one side, it justifies that the ruler adhere to the purity of Islam. That call is to a modest, simple lifestyle, not a lavish one, when Muslims are starving, and wealth defiant of Islam is all about. On the other side, adhering to Islam limits any progress given the conservative Wahhabi establishment's influence over the Saudi royal monarchy. Neil Partrick writes,

> Relying on Islam for a political narrative of legitimacy has often proven to a two-edged sword for the Saudi royal family. Adhering to this vision of "purity" means that religion has served as an anchor of stability but has also turned out to be an obstacle to a modernization and reform. Furthermore, while Islam as a religion has a universal claim, it is at the same time utilized by Saudi monarchs to frame a political narrative of particularistic objectives. First and foremost, for legitimizing and stabilizing the rule of the Al-Saud but also a founding narrative upon which collective identity can be based.[81]

Saudi Arabia claims to protect Islam from impurity, but how would an outsider interpret the revelation, after King Fahd's death, that he had a secret wife named Janan Harb? The arrangement was confirmed in a foreign court of law: "Janan Harb, a socialite who claimed she was the 'secret wife' of the late King Fahd of Saudi Arabia, today won more than £20m in damages and property from his son to continue the 'lavish lifestyle' she had become accustomed to."[82] One should note here that the late king Fahd was the first king to bestow upon himself the title of "Custodian of the Two Holy Mosques." Those who followed him also took the title. Saladin is believed to have been the first person to use the title.[83] He was a Sunni Muslim of Kurdish ethnicity who was the first sultan of Egypt and Syria. He led the Muslim military campaign against the Crusader states in the Levant. At the height of his power, his sultanate included Egypt, Syria, Upper Mesopotamia, the Hejaz, Yemen, and other parts of North Africa.

Many questions arise in view of that story. Is Islam the foundation on which Saudi Arabia draws its power? Does Islam matter when the sovereign decides on domestic and foreign policies? Yes, but *only because* religion serves the kingdom's interests is Saudi Arabia unwilling to relinquish its leadership status in the Muslim world. How could it when Saudi Arabia's existence, its only *political currency*, is based on being *primarily* identified on religious grounds. As stated earlier, there are no political parties, no checks and balances, and so forth in Saudi Arabia; thus, it is challenging to know, in fact, how, and to what degree, the Saudi leadership incorporates religion in its decision making. The outside world sees nothing but a facade that hides behind it a world of contradictions, extravagance, and lifestyles that defy the teachings of Islam. Indeed, the outside world knows not to what degree Saudi Arabia uses Islam since Saudi Arabia disallows polls and surveys that would offer a glimpse into that reality. No surprise there!

Can one even describe Saudi Arabia's foreign policy—if there is one— as Islamic? Hard to say! The reason is that Saudi Arabia uses religion only to serve its interests and further its agenda. For instance, Saudi Arabia's ongoing military ventures in Yemen violate Islamic law. Saudi Arabia, in this scenario, is not rubber-stamping "In the Name of Islam" on this conflict since the KSA knows that the atrocities, the campaign of destruction that Riyadh commits in Yemen *defies* Islam. Recall the Soviet invasion of Afghanistan: Saudi Arabia recruited Mujahedeen from around the Muslim world to fight the Soviets. Every operation, every menial activity conducted in the Afghan theater in that day bore the Islamic stamp. One undoubtedly sees the inconsistency. The religious fiction told by the Saudis allows it to manipulate the Muslim world. It justifies its moral virtues and leadership as grounded in the Qur'an and Islamic law when, in reality, it is not! The only thing that one can conclude with certainty is that religion is an important factor in, and central element of, Saudi identity. Partrick writes:

> Given the centrality of religion in Saudi political narratives, can Saudi foreign policy actually be termed "Islamic foreign policy"? In order to give an answer to this

question one has to keep in mind that Saudi Arabia is *not* a theocratic state even though the Qur'an is characterized as the country's constitution and the kingdom is said to be ruled according to *shariah*. Rather it can be defined more accurately as a monarchy that is to a considerable extent based *on* religion (i.e. the religious element in Saudi political narrative) and based *in* religion (i.e. in a context of highly religious society and environment). Therefore, although religion may not be the primary or single most important factor influencing and determining Saudi foreign policy, it nevertheless remains a factor of high relevance. It is a central element of Saudi (political/ national) *identity* and of the Al-Saudi's narrative of *regime legitimacy*. Religion comes into play in the kingdom's foreign policy whenever these two factors are involved and so it does matter very much.[84]

The Role of Wahhabism

Wahhabism could be the subject of an important book. However, for now, I intend to focus my narrative on how this perverted ideology has served, and continues to serve, as a great source of power for the Al-Saud monarchy. To begin, a *History of Saudi Arabia and Wahhabism*, by Anwar Haroon, provides a detailed factual history of Wahhabism. For now, an easy-to-understand definition of Wahhabism must suffice. Wahhabism is a religious movement founded by Muhammad Ibn Abd al-Wahhab. The movement is described as "ultraconservative," "austere," and "fundamentalist," among other descriptions. Wahhabism has flourished, reaching different parts of the world due to Saudi petrodollars and the kingdom's central influence as protector of Mecca and Medina.

To illuminate this twisted ideology further, Carol Choksy, an adjunct lecturer on strategic intelligence at Indiana University's School of Informatics and Computing, and Jamsheed K. Choksy, a distinguished professor at Indiana University and a member of the US National Council on the Humanities, write:

> The Wahhabi movement that animates Saudi policy from behind the scenes was founded by Muhammad ibn Abd al-Wahhab (1703–92), a Sunni theologian who called for a return to austere practices supposedly followed by the Salaf, or earliest Muslims, during the 7th century. He regarded images, saints, shrines, communal festivals, and secular lifestyles, with music, dance, and socializing, as distractions from true piety. Thus he rejected all changes since early Islam as bid'ah, or heretical innovations and idolatry. He composed the "Kitab al-Tawhid" or "Book of God's Uniqueness," which became the guiding text for his followers, who consequently speak of themselves as Muwahhidun (total monotheists) or as Salafis (followers of the ways of the first Muslims). So as not to detract from those absolutist ideals, they usually do not even refer to themselves as Wahhabis or followers of Wahhab.[85]

Saudi Arabia's devotion to Wahhabism has put it under global scrutiny. Could this ideology be the source of the kingdom's power? I believe so because Wahhabism defines Saudi Arabia's religious identity. The same ideology allows Saudi Arabia to expand its sphere of influence, religiously speaking, for no other reason than self-promoting its image as the guardian of the Islamic faith and a leader of the Muslim world. A few pages follow on the Wahhabist ideology. My objective is to highlight how this ideology not only defines and controls the Saudi society, but also promotes a twisted interpretation of Islam on various issues that have neither been revealed in the Qur'an nor described in the Sunna.

As one who visited the Kingdom of Saudi Arabia many times in an official capacity, I can attest to the influence of its religious establishment, mainly Wahhabist Islam, serving the kingdom as a source of power. Moreover, this is no coincidence given the historical ties between the Al-Saud and Muhammad Ibn Abd al-Wahhab. That relationship, which began during the KSA's inception, prevails to this day. The Wahhabist establishment provides the Al-Saud the religious platform and legitimacy it needs to implement policies and push its agenda forward. That legitimacy not only cements stability for the regime, but also acts as an unchallenged source of power. And how could the Saudi population challenge that when the twisted interpretations of Islam's principles have been drilled into their minds since an early age? How could the Saudi population challenge that when they have been told that the ruling monarchy exists to defend Islam? It is as though Al-Saud have been given some divine authority to subjugate Muslims within and outside Saudi Arabia to the Wahhabist ideology. Those tactics suggest a lack of diversity of thoughts and ideas. I can understand the fear the Wahhabist establishment and the ruling Al-Saud may have if they allow such diversity. Doing so amounts to challenging the misconception about what Islam *says* versus what the Wahhabist clerics *advocate*.

The relationship between Al-Saud and the Wahhabist establishment extends even beyond the borders of Saudi Arabia. Besides the propagation of Wahhabism in different regions of the Muslim world (Pakistan, Sudan, Nigeria, Niger, Indonesia, and Afghanistan), the ideology also reaches other countries in Europe and beyond: Finland, Germany, Albania, New Zealand, and the United States, among others. This propagation is facilitated by petrodollars or, as author Sandra Mackey terms it, "Petro-Islam."[86] This massive undertaking by the Saudi government started back in the 1970s when Riyadh devoted a large part of its oil wealth to further this religious venture. Robert Lacey, a British historian and biographer, writes, "The Kingdom's seventy or so embassies around the world already featured cultural, educational, and military attaches, along with consular officers who organized visas for the hajj. Now they were joined by religious attaches, whose job was to get new mosques built in their countries and to persuade existing mosques to propagate the dawah wahhabiya."[87] With that in mind, one realizes how Saudi Arabia pushed forward to establish and fund different social and financial organizations to advance its agenda, domestically and globally. For instance, the establishment of the Organization of the Islamic Conference, in 1969, later renamed the Organization of the Islamic Cooperation (OIC), was originally based on the idea of unity among Muslims, protection of Islamic holy sites, improvement of economic cooperation, and so forth. Yet, the organization, according to Hady Amr, Director of the Brookings Doha Center, has made little impact on the daily lives of Muslims.[88] The other organization is the Muslim World League (MWL) established in 1962 and headquartered in the holy city of Medina. Two of MWL's objectives are (1) to clarify the true message of Islam and (2) to refute suspicious and false allegations made against the religion. But where is MWL as Rohingya Muslims in Myanmar face genocide under the watchful eyes of Nobel Peace Prize winner Aung San Suu Kyi? Where is MWL as Muslims in Yemen endure famine and unprecedented destruction at the hands of Saudi Arabia and its Arab coalition? Examples abound! Interestingly, Saudi Arabia funds both the OIC and MWL, which seem to embody and reinforce Saudi Arabia's self-conception of being Islam's guardians and the leaders of the Muslim world.[89]

Readers need to fathom that the use of religion is an integral part of Saudi Arabia's domestic and foreign agenda. A tension exists between the Al-Saud and the Wahhabist establishment, though it remains under wraps. Suffice it to say, the Saudi government fully understands that it *cannot* and *will not* challenge the religious establishment. Doing so amounts to declaring a social or religious war, as the Wahhabi clerics will mobilize their supporters to revolt. The Al-Saud will avoid that outcome at any cost. Although that may be a bad-case scenario, I believe the Al-Saud monarchy understands the importance of maintaining peace with the religious establishment in return for the regime's stability and legitimacy. One must stress that, from time to time, tensions between the Saudi leadership and the religious establishment erupt. Those tensions are over social issues such as granting more freedoms for the Saudis or deciding the clerical establishment's exact role within the leadership hierarchy. Neil Partrick writes,

> The tension between the clerical role and the Al-Saud state interest was marked after 9/11. On the one hand the head of the MWL, Sheikh Abdullah Al-Turki, was deployed by the Saudi state to push a message of inter-faith tolerance and condemnation of all terrorism conducted in the name if Islam. On the other, he angered at least two senior Saudi princes, Prince Turki Al-Faisal (the then

recently retired head of foreign intelligence) and Prince Talal bin Abdulaziz (a half-brother of the then king), by arguing that the ulema were partners in power. Both princes publicly rebuffed this suggestion. Abdullah Al-Turki might have been intending to emphasise that the precise role of the ulema had been one of support ever since the alliance of Mohammed bin Abdul-Wahhab and Mohammed bin Saud. Prince Turki Al-Faisal argued that official clerics, who are, by definition state employees, should be precisely that – it is the government that governs and clerics should adhere to state interests.[90]

Clearly, Wahhabism is one of the sources of Saudi Arabia's political power. I strongly believe that the relationship between Al-Saudi and the Wahhabist establishment will not be permanently abandoned. Nevertheless, current domestic and global dynamics are forcing the government of Saudi Arabia to reconsider the extent of its ties with Wahhabist clerics. This relationship with Wahhabism is now under global scrutiny, and many around the world, including Muslims, are blaming the Saudi government for funding terrorism and allowing it to propagate inside and outside of its borders. That promulgation is due to the Saudi government allowing Wahhabist clerics to circulate twisted interpretations of Islam. So, when we hear rhetoric coming out of Riyadh that condemns terrorism, it is nothing but a window dressing that masks a much darker reality. Consider the following, "*The Grand Mufti of Saudi Arabia, condemned Islamic State of* Iraq and the Levant (Isil), insisting, 'the ideas of extremism, radicalism and terrorism do not belong to Islam in any way.' Somewhat paradoxically, however, members of the Saudi ruling class have applauded Wahhabism for its Salafi piety i.e., its adherence to the original practices of Islam and the movement's vehement opposition to the Shia branch of Islam."[91]

However, we are starting to see signs of fracture in the relationship between the Al-Saud monarchy and the religious establishment. For instance, King Salman recently issued a royal decree to lift the ban on women driving in Saudi Arabia. The royal decree, in my opinion, sends a strong message that the monarchy can forego consulting with the religious establishment when making decisions. But I say not so fast. Lifting the ban on women driving does not entail that the Al-Saud are going to marginalize the religious establishment permanently. The relationship was developed over millennia, and it will take a long time for it to cease to exist—if it ever does.

To provide readers with a perspective of how powerful the Wahhabi establishment has been over decades, consider the following narrative from Mohammed Rasooldeen and Rashid Hassan. King Abdulaziz sought the approval of the religious establishment when he wanted to introduce the radio into Saudi Arabia. However, the religious establishment ruled that the radio and telegraph should be banned. The king supported that decision and forbade radio use for a period. Similarly, the religious establishment also played an important role in the power struggle that broke out between King Saud and his brother Faisal. The then Grand Mufti of the KSA, Sheikh Mohammed bin Ibrahim Al-Sheikh, issued a fatwa calling for the removal of King Saud, who was succeeded by his brother Faisal and who ruled from 1964 to 1975. The latter was assassinated in 1975 by his nephew Faisal bin Musaid. However, the monarchy's supporters argue that recent developments in Saudi Arabia indicate the imminent divorce of the political establishment (Al-Saud) from the religious (Wahhabi) establishment. I remain skeptical, however, given Crown Prince MbS's recent pledge that Saudi Arabia will return to what it was before, a country of moderate Islam open to all religions and to the world.[92] Based on my historical knowledge of the country, Saudi Arabia has never adopted moderate Islam. That is unlike Morocco and Jordan, two monarchies that continue to strike a balance between their Islamic identity and modernity.

Saudi Arabia has used religion thus far to achieve its local, regional, and global objectives, be they involvement in proxy wars and establishment of religious madrassas around the world or funding governments and organizations to support Saudi Arabia's policies. Whatever the case may be, the discovery of oil also proves to be another great source of power Saudi Arabia relies significantly upon. After all, global economies depend heavily on oil imports, especially from a country that is bountiful in this black gold commodity. In the nineteenth century, one would never have dreamt that such massive wealth could come from a tribe of Bedouins, but that is the story of Saudi Arabia today.

Oil: A Source of Power

Most agree on this fact: If it were not for oil, we would not be talking much about Saudi Arabia. The desert kingdom would be one of those forgotten countries, lost in the pages of history and trashed in its dustbin. However, reality is that oil exists in Saudi Arabia. Because of its massive oil wealth, Saudi Arabia today wields an economic influence as it sits on proven oil reserves of 266 billion barrels, according to Saudi government estimates. That estimate seems questionable to me. Although I cannot definitely confirm those estimates, my objective is not to discuss how many barrels of oil Saudi Arabia produces. Rather, my purpose is to explain how Saudi Arabia uses oil as another source of its power. Oil production in Saudi Arabia has transformed the country from a cluster of tribes and Bedouins to a country that influences global oil prices and tilts the global economy toward success or failure. At least that was the case a few decades ago. Geopolitical realities have changed dramatically so that Saudi Arabia's influence seems to be waning. To illustrate, in 2016, estimates issued by Rystad Energy, an independent oil and gas consulting firm, suggest that the United States holds more oil reserves than Saudi Arabia. Their estimate puts the recoverable oil at about 264 billion barrels. Given those estimates, one wonders how long the oil beneath the desert sands in Saudi Arabia will last. In the last decade or so, more and more energy experts are starting to focus their analyses on the US energy market and how it could shift the power play in the global energy market. Anjli Raval, oil and gas correspondent, writes, "'There is little potential for future surprises in many other countries, but in the US there is,' said Per Magnus Nysveen, analyst at Rystad Energy, noting recent discoveries in the Permian Basin in Texas and New Mexico, which is the nation's most prolific oil producing area. 'Three years ago the US was behind Russia, Canada and Saudi Arabia.'"[93]

The lifting of sanctions on Iran, the fifth-largest oil producer in the world, will only contribute to the decline of Saudi Arabia's economic influence on the global stage. However, as I stated earlier, this narrative is not about the *quantity* of Saudi oil reserves. Rather, it is about how Saudi Arabia is using oil wealth to control its population, secure its firm grip on power, and purchase loyalties from inside and outside the kingdom. In essence, oil has become the tool whereby the Al-Saud monarchy can subject the Saudi population to its will. Further, oil became the revenue base on which the Saudi royal family not only funds its lavish lifestyle, but also controls its population. As with religion, the Al-Saud figured out early that using oil as a political-economic tool could steer the country into the path of obedience and unquestionable loyalty. That in turn would cement a lavish lifestyle for a monarchy that contradicts Islam's proscriptions. Let there be no illusion: Saudi Arabia has flourished because of the improvements that oil revenue makes possible. The accumulation of massive oil wealth made it possible for Al-Saud to enter into a social contract with its people whereby the Saudi government (Al-Saud family) funds all social programs in return for the population's loyalty. Neil Partrick writes, "The fact that Saudi Arabia has been capitalized upon its abundant resource base has enabled the state to accrue enormous financial resources, accelerate the pace of development within the country and perpetuate its governing structures. Furthermore, it has enabled a social contract whereby the state provides everything for everything and society supposedly wants for nothing; in return, society acquiesces to the authority of the state. Thus, oil, the mainstay of budget revenues, is also the source of stability."[94]

I believe the discovery of oil and the wealth it generates allow the Saudi government to make its people dependent on the state for their economic and social needs. It is one thing to have the government provide certain social services and programs. It is another to render the entire population *completely* dependent on the state. This is a classic example of rentier state theory. To those who are unfamiliar with this concept, the theory, which developed in the political science field, suggests that a rentier state derives all, or a substantial portion, of its national revenues from the rent of indigenous resources (oil, in the case of Saudi Arabia) to external clients. Hossein Mahdavy first postulated this theory, in 1970. Interestingly, not only Saudi Arabia uses this approach, but also other Gulf Cooperation Council (GCC) monarchies (Bahrain, Kuwait, Oman, Qatar, and the UAE) as well. Of note: the Gulf region accounts for more than one-third of the world's explored oil resources. These monarchies have become among the largest oil producers and exporters in the world.

As with Islam, oil can be a two-edged sword for the Al-Saud. On the one hand, the provision of social programs to all Saudis to render them dependent on the state may have passed its shelf life. On the other hand, a growing number of young Saudis is armed with social media platforms. This younger generation not only lust to join the world's technological revolution, but also make different demands that will eventually put pressure on the Saudi government. The monarchy would be wise to ensure that its government has a strategy in place that addresses *specifically* the needs of a growing young population. The Saudi government needs to project the domestic oil consumption for the next 20 to 30 years, so it can plan accordingly. Otherwise, its youth may rebel, and, in an era of social media, it could be challenging for the monarchy to quell demonstrations. The removal of Hosni Mubarak from power in Egypt shows *just* how challenging.

One must understand the psychological impact the monarchy feels any time there is a discussion about changing the kingdom's educational system, its religious outlook, freedom of the press, or political participation. For the reasons listed above, Saudi Arabia can predicate its foreign policy on only limited bases. Arguably, there are a set of values, core national interests, and strategic objectives on which Saudi Arabia bases its policies. Those values are not subject to debate since one person alone, the king, makes the decision in an absolute monarchy. In Saudi Arabia's case, only one set of values and interests matter the most: *survival* of the Al-Saud monarchy. For this reason, oil is the perfect economic, social, and political instrument for the Al-Saud to balance its competing agendas, domestically and globally. Domestically, for instance, Saudi Arabia provides social programs to keep the population silent. Internationally, Saudi Arabia uses oil as a medium to play one party or country off another. Yet, the danger in this approach is that, in the not-so-distant past, clashes between the locals and Saudi forces in the province of Qatif showed how that strategy could go awry.[95] To the chagrin of the West, Saudi Arabia's use of oil to augment its political power indeed affects the world economy. As a result, the West turns a blind eye on human rights abuses, atrocities committed by the Saudi government in the name of Islam, and other violations. Karen Elliott House writes, "Much as many in the West might like to dismiss the Saudis as religious zealots who are reaping the results of Islamic extremism that they set in motion, the decisions of the Al-Saud affect both the economic prosperity of Western societies and, of course, the lives of Western citizens who continue to be targets of radical Islamic terrorists. As a result, the West needs to understand, if not sympathize, with the high-wire act of the Al-Saud amid the changing winds that are buffeting the region and the regime."[96]

To put this within the context of the Al-Saud's firm grip on power, one needs to understand that the billions of dollars Saudi Arabia earns from oil production has allowed it, in the past five or six decades, to assert its power not only domestically but also globally. The use of that power varies depending on location and objective. For instance, when the Arab Spring erupted, in 2011, Saudi Arabia had to react quickly to erect a *fence* against this political tsunami—the Arab Spring. The *fence* consisted of $100 billion in subventions from the Al-Saud family and the promise of 60,000 jobs. That economic bribe may have saved the KSA yesterday, but it may not be enough to meet the demands of growing unemployed Saudi youths tomorrow. The Al-Saud must understand that oil revenues can go only so far. At some point, demand for change becomes the order of the day. The more the state suppresses those demands, the more it tries to silence the population, the louder their voices will become.

Under those circumstances, I see the danger for the Al-Saud in thinking that oil revenues will be adequate means through which Saudi Arabia can address and solve problems. That said, Saudi Arabia' use of Islam and oil as sources of power appears to be ending. The twisted ascetic interpretation of Islam and the funding of Wahhabism contradict Saudi Arabia's actions on the global stage. Said differently, the religious power exhibited through Wahhabism seems to be confronting head-on the much-needed changes segments of the Saudi society demand: jobs, equal rights for women, freedom of the press, minority rights, and religious tolerance. Martin Indyk, executive vice president of the Brookings Institution in Washington, D.C., writes:

> And the Saudi system is fragile. Power is concentrated in the hands of the king and his brothers, who are old and ailing. The Saud family's legitimacy depends in significant part on its pact with a fundamentalist Wahhabi clergy that is deeply opposed to basic political reforms, such as equal rights for women. The deep structural tensions generated

by a 21ˢᵗ-century Westernized elite existing within a 15ᵗʰ-century Saudi social structure have been papered over for decades by oil wealth. If this strange social contract begins to fray, it might tear completely. And over in the eastern quarter, next to Bahrain, where most of Saudi Arabia's oil reserves are located, sits a restive Shiite minority who have been treated as second-class citizens for decades.[97]

Where from here? It all depends on how the Al-Saud monarchy wants to proceed. At some point, the monarchy will have to reflect on itself. The shelf life for Wahhabism's support is expiring; oil reserves will eventually dry out; and new global markets (like those of China) are emerging and will be the next destination. In this scenario, Saudi Arabia will be left with three options. The first is to come up with a new source of power after the oil is depleted. The second is to respond positively and wisely to the demand (creating jobs, building infrastructure for the 21ˢᵗ century, and so on.) of its population, mainly youths. The third is to risk it all by suppressing its population, using whatever means at its disposal. In my opinion, the latter option will put the nail on the royal family's coffins. Yet, if that happens, I caution, it could prove detrimental to the survival of the monarchy and the stability of the state. At that point, it probably would be time to consider a post-Saudi Arabia era.

Although I am an optimist by nature, I offer realistic assessments. Current developments in Saudi Arabia, including the massive crackdown on moderate scholars and religious figures, leads me to wonder about the desert kingdom's ultimate stability. The doubts over Saudi Arabia's stability have been raised consistently and frequently. Rightly so! Saudi Arabia sits on massive oil reserves, and any disruption to the flow of oil due to internal unrest would influence markets worldwide. Instability in Saudi Arabia would definitely destabilize the region exponentially, especially given the other present conflicts in the Middle East.

As of this writing, the Saudi government ordered the arrest of senior princes, including one of the world's richest men, prince Al-Waleed bin Talal, along with former ministerial cabinet members. Those detained were being held at the Ritz Carlton in Riyadh, which had hosted a major investment conference with global business titans from the United States,

Japan, and other countries only days earlier. Do the detentions signal a crack in Saudi Arabia's leadership structure? Do they suggest discontent among members of the royalty about where the kingdom is headed? Alternatively, do the arrests highlight the much-needed change the desert kingdom wants to embark on? Does becoming progressive require first removing obstacles? Interestingly, among those arrested are two of the late king Abdullah's sons. That suggests that the arrest seeks to remove any opposition to Crown Prince MbS's economic Vision 2030. Simultaneously, the arrest also provides MbS the opportunity to cement his authority in dictatorial style. Stephen Kalin and Katie Paul write, "Analysts said the purge aimed to go beyond corruption and aimed to remove potential opposition to Prince Mohammed's ambitious reform agenda which is widely popular with Saudi Arabia's burgeoning youth population but faces resistance from some of the old guard more comfortable with the kingdom's traditions of incremental change and rule by consensus."[98]

I am certain the recent campaign of arrests of royal family members has nothing to do with economics or corruption. Rather, it is MbS's way of silencing his critics, especially the more experienced, elder members from within the royal family. Given the arrests and kidnappings of some of the royal family princes, I am convinced, more than ever, that the future stability of Saudi Arabia, once again, is coming to the fore. The hyperbole about corruption and making the KSA a moderate state is nonsense. Prominent whistle-blower Ali Adubisi, a Saudi in self-exile who heads the Berlin-based European-Saudi Organization for Human Rights, called the crown prince's campaign a "black comedy."[99] Nabih Bulos and Laura King write, "Critics call it a campaign of selective prosecution waged by an indulged young royal prince, MbS with ties to business entities that stand to benefit immensely from the removal of some of those arrested. 'This move is more a matter of organizing corruption,' he said, 'so that it is in the hands of MBS and his coterie.'"[100] Questions of how the young, inexperienced, and impulsive prince, MbS, intends to address domestic issues, let alone challenges of regional and global scope, are urgent. The prince appears to have no strategy or economic formula for moving Vision 2030 forward. What we have heard, thus far, is nothing but empty rhetoric. It is one thing to push, for instance, some form of women's rights. It is another to have a successful economic strategy to create jobs for Saudi youth. Saudi Arabia's unemployment rate is getting higher and higher, and the population has been weaned on cradle-to-grave welfare. It will be dangerous if Al-Saud procrastinates in addressing key domestic issues. Doing so would be a recipe for political and security instability that could spill beyond the borders of the desert kingdom. Paul B. Stares and Helia Ighani write:

> Yet for all the confident assertions that it is just a matter of time before the kingdom succumbs to internal unrest and even regime collapse, Saudi Arabia has remained one of the most stable countries in the region. It has weathered a major downturn in global oil prices and reduction of state revenues, managed what could have been a contentious royal succession, and prosecuted a costly military intervention in neighboring Yemen without facing major domestic blowback, all contrary to the expectations of many outside observers. So is Saudi Arabia the proverbial dog that regularly barks but never bites? Or is there only a false sense of calm for now, before the underlying risks of instability suddenly materialize? Put differently, how worried should we be?[101]

Conclusion

Oil has contributed to rebuilding the Saudi economy as oil revenues provided the KSA the ability to spend on some groups of society generously, including the religious establishment, thus leading to the creation of a system of favoritism and penetration of many social structures, especially tribal and religious ones. The impact of oil revenues lies not in the bilateral relationship between Al-Saud and the religious establishment only. Rather, it extends to include a third element: the governed. Al-Saud understood early on that if they lost the religious establishment, they would have to compete fiercely against it to win over the population. Said differently, oil revenues serve not only as a power tool to exert authority, but also a political and economic medium through which the Al-Saud family controls society.

Interestingly, this authority and the relationship of Al-Saud to its people are facilitated with the mediation of the *religious establishment*.

Saudi Arabia should ask itself if the time has come for self-reflection and reassessment of where it is headed or if it should move forward, forging new alliances by using new sources of power. This debate occurs within the context of the US-Saudi relations, as Saudi Arabia witnesses a major shift in protocol over royal succession. The elevation of Crown Prince MbS to next in line to the throne has already created tensions within the royal family. With that in mind, I wonder what the future of US-Saudi relations may look like in the upcoming years. Chapter 4 addresses this particular relationship in more detail.

CHAPTER IV

US-Saudi Relations: Present and Future

Undoubtedly, one cannot cover the entire history of US-Saudi relations in a few pages. However, one must briefly illuminate the historical evolution of this important, complex relationship. I believe even my brief narrative of the approximately eight decades of involvement by fourteen US presidents helps one to understand the relations playing out today. However, my focus remains to explain the importance of this crucial, complex, volatile, and evolutionary US-Saudi relationship given the geopolitical, economic, and social changes occurring in the Middle East today.

At the turn of the 20th century, the United States' engagement in the greater Middle East was minimal. In fact, historical records indicate that Great Britain, a formidable power at that time, took the lead. During this era, British leaders ordered British soldiers to land in the southern city of Basra, Iraq, to defend oil supplies from Persian aggression. During that period, the United States neither pursued an aggressive policy with regard to oil production in the Middle East nor desired to conquer the region. In fact, the United States focused its interests, during that time, on Latin America and the Pacific.

US-Saudi relations should be placed within the context of the Middle East's evolving political and economic changes. Doing so provides readers a clear understanding of why, behind the scenes, the United States' policy toward the Middle East has to go through the gates of Saudi Arabia.

Chronologically, the US-Saudi relationship started in 1933 when full diplomatic relations between the US and Saudi Arabia were established. My historical reference point starts with President Franklin D. Roosevelt

(FDR) in the early 1940s. More specifically, I consider that the decades' long alliance between Saudi Arabia and the United States officially started, in 1945.

The Franklin D. (FDR) Roosevelt Administration (1933–1945) 32nd President of the US

The events and politics of World War II marked the era of the Roosevelt administration. During that time, the United States' need for oil became a priority. FDR not only recognized and understood this reality, but also saw an opportunity for how WW II could make it possible for the United States to extend its influence over the Middle East. FDR's move aimed to secure access to oil in response to America's growing demands and challenge, possibly even undermine, Europe's influence in the Middle East. As a result, FDR was perceived as one who made it possible for subsequent US administrations to expand America's influence and foster a new political order, one in which the Kingdom of Saudi Arabia became the center as oil for security became the pillar of US-Saudi relations for decades to come.

Saudi Arabia discovered oil in its eastern region with the assistance of Standard Oil of California, now Chevron. The discovery allowed Saudi Arabia to be perceived as a key player in Middle Eastern politics. FDR wanted to capitalize immediately on that when he admitted to being "greatly interested" in building a strategic partnership with Saudi Arabia.[102] Against this backdrop, the rise of Saudi Arabia, due to its massive undeveloped oil fields, shifted the FDR administration's focus to perceiving the desert kingdom as a valuable strategic partner. Thus, FDR based his conclusion on his ability to realize the potential for Saudi Arabia to play a crucial role during the war efforts due to its strategic location and oil wealth.

While discussing the arrangements of the distribution of the "Lend Lease" to Saudi Arabia would make an interesting topic, suffice it to state that FDR understood the pivotal role the KSA could play during WW II and in subsequent years. Being the shrewd politician he was, FDR bestowed praise and admiration on Saudi Arabia despite those sorts of accolades usually being reserved for more important wartime allies such as the then Soviet Union.

In an effort to promote US-Saudi relations, FDR initiated discussions with Ibn Saud about forging a military partnership. The dialog resulted in establishing a US military air base in Saudi Arabia. The invitation extended to two of Abdul Aziz Ibn Saud's sons, princes Faisal and Khalid, to visit Washington, in 1943, cemented US-Saudi relations.[103] Each prince later became King of the KSA. Once WW II concluded, in 1945, it became evident to not only FDR but also other American officials that Saudi Arabia would help to advance American strategic interests afterward. Thus, Saudi Arabia was granted a special status as the emerging pro-American state in the Middle East.

The Harry S. Truman Administration (1945–1952): 33rd President of the US

Historians agree that President Truman's tenure in the White House witnessed a shift in policy trajectory that would influence US foreign policy toward the Middle East for decades to come. This policy focused mainly on protecting Iranian oil fields from any foreign aggression in addition to addressing the transfer of military supplies to the USSR. However, after President Truman threatened to use force against the Soviet military presence in Iran, Stalin withdrew his forces. Truman's foreign-policy declaration marked the beginning of American foreign policy toward the greater Middle East. Truman's strategic vision for the region extended beyond small gains. Rather, his political calculations included establishing a treaty of sorts with Mohammed Reza Shah Pahlavi. According to historians, this move marked the beginning of confrontation with the USSR over ideological dominance and expansion in the greater Middle East.[104]

Political events in the Middle East unfolded quickly after WW II. The North Atlantic Treaty Organization (NATO) invited Turkey to join, and the United Nations helped to establish the state of Israel, which Truman recognized 11 minutes after its creation, on May 14, 1948. Those events highlight the fast-changing political dynamics in the Middle East early on. While the emergence of Israel on the Middle East's political scene was a monumental and highly debated event, my focus remains on how the relationship between Saudi Arabia and the United States evolved under the Truman administration. In 1950, the US State Department received an unusual request from its ambassador to Saudi Arabia. According to Taylor Kate Brown, the request reads, "HM has requested our assistance in obtaining the immediate services of an outstanding specialist, who with an assistant could go to Saudi Arabia to examine and treat him for chronic osteoarthritis from which he is becoming increasingly uncomfortable and enfeebled."[105]

President Truman agreed to send his personal physician, Brigadier General Wallace H. Graham, along with a medical team charged with looking over the Saudi king. As the US medical team made its final preparations, the Saudi government sent a request through its ambassador to Washington asking Truman to disallow all news coverage regarding the medical team's upcoming visit to the kingdom on April 15, 1950.[106] Consequently, President Truman's justification for keeping the medical team's trip to Saudi Arabia secret had to do with (a) Saudi Arabia's ties with Aramco's oil, and (b) the US government's strong anticommunist views. Truman understood that approving the secret mission would serve his political interests in the long term. He was right. Secretary of State Dean Acheson stated that Ibn Saud was touched by Truman's gesture in sending his personal physician. The trip was also a diplomatic success, which made possible the mutual defense agreement between the United States and the Kingdom of Saudi Arabia. Interestingly, this agreement was the basis of the US-Saudi military cooperation that continues to prevail today despite periods of tension between Washington and Riyadh.

The Dwight D. Eisenhower Administration (1953-1961): 34th President of the US

The Eisenhower administration faced three major events: in 1953, the ousting of the popular Iranian leader, Mohamed Mosaddeq in 1956, France, Britain, and Israel attacked Egypt after the latter decided to nationalize the Suez Canal; and, in 1958, President Eisenhower ordered US troops into Beirut to protect the Lebanese Christian-led government.

In the wake of the events of 1953, President Eisenhower sought to stabilize the Middle East. Yet, in the opinion of many historians, he was mistaken to have courted Gamal Abdel Nasser of Egypt. Eisenhower's decision to make Egypt a regional security partner in the hope of enticing Nasser to join the West in the Cold War efforts proved to be a strategic mistake. Nevertheless, President Eisenhower exerted pressure on his allies, mainly Great Britain, to the point of bringing the latter's economy to the brink of destruction.[107]

What marked the Eisenhower era is the latter's policy toward Saudi Arabia under King Ibn Saud, in 1953. King Ibn Saud led his country into a lucrative oil industry, turning Saudi Arabia from a cluster of tribes into a wealthy nation. A partnership with the American oil firm Chevron facilitated the transition. However, Ibn Saud's death set off a succession rivalry between his sons Saud and Faisal. Without detailing what happened because of that rivalry, suffice it to state that the Eisenhower administration helped to diffuse tensions between Britain and Saudi Arabia over the Buraimi Oasis, an oil-rich territory in southeastern Arabia. By doing so, Eisenhower preserved his relationship with both Britain and Saudi Arabia.

The John F. Kennedy Administration (1961– 1963): 35th President of the US

The Kennedy administration desired to improve Eisenhower's deteriorated relations with Arab nationalists by strengthening ties with Arabs and Israel. By doing so, President Kennedy signaled to the Arab world his willingness to have an honest debate about mutual concerns and shared interests. Further, the distrust between Saudi Arabia and the United States, mostly because of US foreign policies or its absence during the Egypt-Saudi proxy war, became more palpable.

During the Kennedy administration, Saudi Arabia was dealing with a host of issues, including internal royal infighting, threats of revolution, and civil unrest. During this period, Saudi Arabia was lagging behind in education, skilled workers, and a well-trained, well-structured military establishment. Likewise, the Kennedy era witnessed an internal conflict in Yemen that transformed into a proxy war between Egypt and Saudi Arabia. The conflict created fear and anxiety within the Saudi monarch, knowing how much Gamal Abdel Nasser wanted to "crush the authority of the Saudi Arabian Government."[108]

During his short tenure, President Kennedy tried to push Saudi Arabia into undertaking meaningful domestic reforms. Kennedy based his thinking on his administration's advice that providing military support to Saudi Arabia might prove ineffective. President Kennedy was convinced that Saudi Arabia needed to undergo domestic reforms that could counter the Arab nationalism headed, at that time, by Nasser.

Most historians agree that the Kennedy administration's approach to not only Saudi Arabia but also the greater Middle East sought to ensure that countries in the region did not fall prey to the communist USSR. Kennedy's rapprochement to Nasser's Egypt was mainly for that purpose and that purpose only. Similarly, Kennedy saw the need to not only sustain a relationship with Saudi Arabia, but also develop it. He rationalized that vast oil resources were not only making Saudi Arabia wealthier, but also allowing it to claim leadership in the Muslim world for being home to the two holiest sites in Islam, Mecca and Medina. Note that President Kennedy's containment policy toward Soviet communism, at least within the confinement of the Middle East, was facilitated through Israel and Saudi Arabia. Antonio Perra comments that "The Saudi's in particular were increasingly viewed as 'an atavistic regime who would soon disappear' but Kennedy's support for them-which hardened during the Yemen Crisis even as he sought to placate Nasser-had the unintended effect of making them, as today, the US's great pillar of support in the Middle East."[109]

The Lyndon B. Johnson Administration (1963–1968): 36th President of the US

President Johnson assumed the US presidency following Kennedy's assassination, in November 1963. Major domestic and global events marked LBJ's tenure in the White House. Those events included the

Vietnam War, the Great Society for America, and the End to Poverty and Racial Injustice.

President Johnson's policy toward the Middle East, in general, and the Kingdom of Saudi Arabia, in particular, was tested during the Six Day War of 1967, in which Egypt, Syria, and Jordan attacked Israel. The attack compelled the US to intervene due to the special US-Israeli relations. The Six Day War of 1967 consumed much of President Johnson's political energy toward the Middle East. Yet, Johnson wanted to distance himself from his predecessor's call for political and economic reforms. Therefore, President Johnson ordered the US Ambassador to Saudi Arabia at that time, Hermann F. Elits, to stop advocating for reforms to the Saudi king. The Johnson administration argued that Saudi Arabia knew what was best for its interests and could handle its own affairs accordingly. President Johnson's subsequent policy toward Saudi Arabia involved arms sales, a continuation of Kennedy's policy. Johnson's military sales between 1962 and 1964 to both Saudi Arabia and Iran doubled, and they continued to increase over the course of the Johnson's administration and beyond.[110]

The Richard M. Nixon Administration (1969-1974): 37th President of the US

The Watergate scandal was the dark stain on the white page of Nixon's presidential history. Yet, the diplomatic efforts of Nixon and Secretary of State Henry Kissinger defined US relations with some major powers during the 1970s. However, President Nixon faced a serious economic challenge resulting from the oil embargo Saudi Arabia imposed on the US in retaliation for supporting Israel during the 1973 October war. Colossal economic devastation followed from the embargo: oil prices soared, long lines formed at gas stations, and the KSA received massive transfers of wealth. The embargo placed a heavy burden on not only the United States but also other governments. Neither corporations nor motorists around the world were spared. Neff, a journalist and author, wrote, "'The embargo,' Henry A. Kissinger later admitted, had 'the most drastic consequences' for the United States, adding, 'It increased our unemployment and contributed to the deepest recession we have had in the postwar [World War II] period.'

What Kissinger failed to say was that he bore major responsibility for the boycott."[111] However, Kissinger's statement about Saudi Arabia in the aftermath of the oil embargo shed light on how Washington perceived Saudi Arabia at that time. Mirzadegan writes, "He [Kissinger] thought of Saudi Arabia as little more than a sparsely populated country that happened to have large oil reserves; it was not a nation suited for a major/important role on the world stage like Iran. Even before the embargo in May 1973, Kissinger stated to Deputy Secretary of Defense Bill Clements, 'We wouldn't give a damn about Saudi Arabia if it didn't have most of the oil in the region.'"[112] Suffice it to state that (a) Nixon and his secretary of state, Kissinger, missed the opportunity to prevent the prolonged rise of oil prices and (b) failed to put pressure on Iran, which, at that time, could have increased its oil production.

In a nutshell, the Nixon administration, and eventually President Ford's as well, failed to prevent Saudi and Iranian leaders from pressuring American consumers in return for providing a buffer against Soviet encroachment in the Middle East. The Nixon administration's grand strategy and Cold War politics took precedence over domestic economic and energy-supply problems.

The Gerald R. Ford Jr. Administration (Aug. 1974-Jan. 1977): 38th President of the US

President Ford started his presidency with US-Soviet relations on shaky ground. However, the 1973 Yom Kippur War in the Middle East had nearly led to the massive military involvement of the superpowers. Moreover, throughout 1973 and 1974, the Soviets grew increasingly frustrated with several US politicians—mainly Senator Henry "Scoop" Jackson (D-WA)—who had successfully tied American trade with the Soviets to the relaxation of Soviet emigration policies. Perhaps unsurprisingly, then, American relations with the Soviets during the Ford years witnessed notable failures as well as successes.

The James (Jimmy) E. Carter, Jr. Administration (1977–1981): 39th President of the US

Historians agree that the Carter administration's policies toward the Middle East, in general, and Saudi Arabia, in particular, experienced both success and failure. On the one hand, the Carter administration's tenacity, mediation, and negotiations of the Camp David Accord in 1978 made possible a peace agreement between Israel and Egypt and was signed, in 1979. On the other hand, the Carter administration failed to secure the release of US hostages at the US embassy in Tehran in the aftermath of the Iranian revolution, in 1979. The hostage crisis lasted 444 days until Ronald Reagan's election as president. The Carter administration channeled some of its policies toward the Middle East through Saudi Arabia for various reasons. For instance, during the Iran-Iraq War, President Carter loaned four sophisticated airborne warning and control system (AWACS) aircraft and their crews to Saudi Arabia to monitor war developments between Iraq and Iran. Consequently, Saudi Arabia started to think seriously about acquiring advanced US weaponry, building a military infrastructure, and constructing a modern military apparatus. However, the Iranian revolution prompted the Carter administration to persuade Congress to authorize the sale of enhanced US military weaponry to the desert kingdom. The Carter administration argued that the Saudis needed US military hardware to protect its oil fields from the newly emerged Iranian hardliners in Tehran.

During the Carter administration, Saudi Arabia reversed course by selling oil to the US for far cheaper than other countries would. Saudi Arabia sold oil to the US for $6-7 per barrel less in order to help Carter's bid for reelection. Unfortunately, for the Saudis, their economic maneuvering failed, and Carter lost his reelection bid to Ronald Reagan.

The Ronald W. Reagan Administration (1981–1989): 40th President of the US

Major events happened during the Reagan years. Israel invaded Lebanon, in 1982. The Iran-Contra scandal broke, in 1986. Bombings in

Beirut killed 241 American soldiers, in 1983, and John Hinckley tried to assassinate Reagan himself, in 1988.

It was, however, the special relationship the Reagan administration developed with Saudi Arabia under the leadership of the late king Fahd that shaped America's foreign policy toward not only the desert kingdom but also the greater Middle East. The common objective of this relationship converged on one major theme: the defeat of communism. Both Saudi Arabia and the Reagan administration joined forces in their crusade by supporting anticommunist fighters, be they in Africa and the Middle East or central Asia and Latin America. King Fahd understood early on the need to help finance Reagan's efforts to defeat communism. In support of those efforts, the Saudi leadership diverted petrodollars to help Washington, expecting to win favors in return. Thus, the Saudis funded the Mujahedeen in Afghanistan against the Soviets and provided money to the National Union for the Total Independence of Angola (UNITA).

Historians agree that the Reagan administration strongly advocated for the sale of modern American weapons to Saudi Arabia. The relationship President Reagan and King Fahd enjoyed traces its roots back to the 1970s when the KSA played a pivotal role in reversing Egypt's position, pulling it from the Soviet Union's orbit and into the United States'. Similarly, Saudi Arabia funded the airlifting of Moroccan troops to Zaire, in 1977, to save the Mobutu regime from Katangan secessionist forces. One must highlight the role of the Saudi ambassador at that time, Prince Bandar. The prince had major access in Washington and helped Saudi Arabia provide the Contras with at least $32 million to keep their counterrevolution alive. Interestingly, in 1981, Bandar stated, "If you knew what we really were doing for America, you wouldn't just give us AWACS, you would give us nuclear weapons."[113]

Misjudgment and limited vision guided some of President Reagan's foreign-policy failures in the Middle East, thus yielding unwanted outcomes. For instance, the Reagan administration assumed that supporting Saddam Hussein in his war against Iran would guarantee Iraq's victory. To President Reagan's dismay, Iraq was unable to defeat Iran and the strong will of its people.

The George H. W. Bush Administration (1989–1993): 41st President of the US

Historians agree that Iraq's invasion of Kuwait in 1991 shaped the Bush administration's foreign policy toward both the Middle East and Saudi Arabia. The Bush administration's rationale for gathering a coalition to drive out Iraqi forces from Kuwait stemmed from the serious threat Saddam posed to the security of Saudi Arabia, the flow of oil to the US, and America's overall interests in the region.

However, the Saudis mistrusted America's intentions after the US established military bases on Saudi soil. The United Nations' coalition drove Saddam's forces out of Kuwait. The role the Bush administration played in leading that coalition not only restored pride, morale, and status for the United States as a global leader, but also put things in perspective for Saudi Arabia. Without the United States guaranteeing security, the desert kingdom would become vulnerable, thereby risking its political, economic, and security stability.

President Bush's foreign policy is associated with the term "New World Order." That new thinking led the Bush administration to deemphasize Cold War alliances and stand firmly against rogue nations. Since then, it has been a back-and-forth debate regarding whether the Bush administration's victory achieved by driving Iraqi forces from Kuwait had the desired results. Opponents argue that Bush did not actually win since Saddam Hussein remained in power in Iraq after withdrawing his forces from Kuwait. In 2003, and subsequently, others argued that George H. W. Bush's questionable victory was the reason his son, George W. Bush, became president: to finish the job his dad had started. Therefore, the second invasion of Iraq began, in 2003, under the false assumption that it was stockpiling weapons of mass destruction and disguising production capabilities.

The William J. Clinton Administration (1993–2001): 42nd President of the US

Historians suggest that relations between the United States and Saudi Arabia declined during the Clinton administration. The changes did not necessarily result from Clinton himself. The Cold War ended. New states once within the Soviets' orbit became independent. The fall of Soviet communism made Saudi Arabia less important in the eyes of the US since its Cold War considerations lessened in the Middle East. Nevertheless, of all events, the Clinton administration's preoccupation with the Arab-Israeli conflict caused the biggest decline in US-Saudi relations. President Clinton made an Arab-Israeli peace the key feature of his foreign-policy initiative toward the greater Middle East. His efforts were deemed successful when he took credit for mediating the 1994 peace treaty between Israel and Jordan.

Equally important, the US domestic agenda, especially strengthening the US economy, kept President Clinton from engaging more with Saudi Arabia. Both the US and Saudi Arabia had their own justifications of what contributed to the relationship's decline. Saudi Arabia, for example, risked being perceived as "cozying up" to the Americans; even the *perception* could have serious repercussions in Saudi Arabia. As a result, the close relationship became justification for terrorists to carry out activities against both the US and Saudi Arabia. Despite the decline in US-Saudi relations during President Clinton's tenure, the rise of international terrorism made Saudi Arabia more vulnerable and "increased the regime's sense of vulnerability and hence its inclination to seek protection from the United States."[114]

The George W. Bush Administration (2001–2009): 43rd President of the US

The election of George W. Bush ushered in a new era for US-Saudi relations and introduced new challenges. The 9/11 attacks on New York City and the Pentagon were wrathful and devastating; what made the attacks especially problematic for the Saudis is that 15 of the 19 hijacker-attackers were Saudi nationals.

Three main events defined President George W. Bush's tenure in office. First, a US-led coalition toppled the Taliban in Afghanistan following the terrorist attacks of September 11, 2001. Second is the ill-conceived invasion of Iraq, in 2003, that resulted in much of the political chaos the Middle East experiences today. Third, President Bush's attempts to mediate between the Palestinians and the Israelis failed miserably.

The 9/11 terrorist attacks compelled President Bush to adopt the "War on Terror" doctrine. However, many analysts questioned why he ignored the Saudis, who had been implicated in the funding and support of some of the terrorists involved in the 9/11 attacks. While a majority of the American people received Bush's January 2002 State of the Union address positively, analysts argue that the speech also delineated the infamous "Axis of Evil" countries consisting of North Korea, Iraq, and Iran, but omitted Saudi Arabia. As a result, President Bush sent a message that Saudi Arabia remained a US ally in the Middle East. By not challenging the Saudis, Mr. Bush's credibility suffered terribly. Many may not know that the Saudi lobby in Washington has the power to silence many, including members of the US congress. The Saudi lobby can persuade congresspeople to forego investigations.

The election of President George W. Bush brought back members of his father's administration. Recall that Dick Cheney, Colin Powell, and Donald H. Rumsfeld also served in the younger Bush's national security team. Cheney held the vice presidency, Powell served as secretary of state, and Rumsfeld worked as secretary of defense. Their long, well-established relationships and experience with the Saudis helped US-Saudi relations weather the storm of 9/11. The US and Saudis thus went on to foster a new era of cooperation against terrorism.

The Barack H. Obama Administration (2009–2017): 44th President of the US

Historians agree that President Obama oversaw an ambiguous, indistinct foreign policy toward the Middle East. Even his relations with

Saudi Arabia were strained at times. The reasons, I argue, reflect a host of factors, including the violence surging in Iraq, the revival of Shi'ites across the region, and the rise in anti-US sentiment across the Muslim world. Yet, Iran's nuclear program placed the strained US-Saudi relations under a global reality check. It is fair to state that Obama's foreign-policy approach recalled that of Woodrow Wilson. Indeed, some of Obama's policy toward the region favored Iran over Saudi Arabia, changing the paradigm and, with it, the regional balance of power.

As stated earlier, Iran's nuclear agreement with the West lay at the heart of US-Saudi tensions during the later Obama years. Arguments within think tanks and among global-affairs analysts suggest that Obama *inherently* distrusted the Saudis. Yet, the Iran nuclear agreement should not be construed as Obama's wanting to *take revenge* on the Saudis. That said, the deal achieved something valuable for Saudi Arabia's enemy, Iran. The deal allowed Iran further to expand its sphere of influence in the region on multiple fronts: economic, military, and ideological. This new narrative led the Saudis to believe that the Obama administration deliberately sought to shift the regional balance of power to Iran. That became even more evident when the Syrian civil war broke out, and the US decided not to intervene. The US's absence created a vacuum that Russia and Iran later filled.

As I argued in the *Volatile State: Iran in the Nuclear Age*, whether the US made a strategic mistake by reaching an agreement with Iran over its nuclear program is yet to be determined. Iran's nuclear deal on Obama's watch has certainly changed geopolitical calculations for Saudi Arabia, which made it possible for Iran to oppose Saudi Arabia's goals and thereby attempt to attain a regional hegemony. Saudi Arabia is marred in its own failed military operations in neighboring Yemen. Under those circumstances, Saudi Arabia cannot truthfully claim to have control over events in the Middle East and therefore cannot claim to have the mantle of regional leader.

Some good things came to US-Saudi relations under President Obama. He approved more than $115 billion in sales of weapons, military equipment, and training to Saudi Arabia. This sale was the most by any U.S. administration in the 71-year U.S.-Saudi alliance.[115]

The Donald J. Trump, Jr. Administration (2017-Present): 45th President of the US

Despite his lack of foreign-policy acumen, President Trump's policies toward the Middle East strike me as no different from those of his predecessor, President Obama. As a result, Trump, thus far, has avoided any military engagement in the Middle East despite the bravado one hears, the tweets one reads, and the leaked statements that emerge from time to time. Trump's May 2017 trip to Saudi Arabia was his first foreign trip as president, and it cast doubt on his ability to fathom the real issues in the Muslim world. Further, the speech he gave from Riyadh was met with low expectations throughout the Muslim world given his lack of credibility, garbled messages, and inconsistencies. That is expected. After all, during his campaign, candidate Trump remarked, "I think Islam hates us."[116]

I believe Saudi Arabia realized Trump naïveté when it used him to deliver what is essentially *Saudi Arabia's* message to Iran. Trump's rhetoric serves Saudi Arabia by helping it to counter Iran's growing regional influence. Yet, Trump failed to address the Saudis' need to rein in Wahhabism and limit its twisted, extremist interpretation of Islam.

So far, relations between Saudi Arabia and its patron, the US, are improving. How long will that last? It is anyone's guess. Trump convinced the Saudis to purchase $110 billion of weapons, though the US Department of Defense refused to confirm the sale. Regardless, purchases of that scale could precipitate an arms race in the region.[117] Only a few weeks later, Iran announced its intention to purchase weapons from China and Russia. Similarly, Turkey purchased Russia's S400 advanced air-to-surface missile systems. With the Saudi purchase of US weapons, Riyadh hopes for something in return: i.e., the repeal of a contentious 2016 law that allows relatives of 9/11 victims to sue Saudi Arabia for the deaths of their loved ones. As of this writing, Saudi Arabia looks more vulnerable than ever. Moreover, Trump is utterly mistaken if he thinks he can influence events on the ground in the Middle East. For now, Trump's naiveté appears to be leading him on a fool's errand of gamely doing the Saudis' dirty work. Such a policy does not serve America or its national interests, only the Saudis'.[118]

The preceding narrative discussed the nature of US-Saudi relations in the context of different US administrations. In closing, I must emphasize the urgency whereby one needs to evaluate where this relationship is headed as geopolitical events in the Middle East unfold. Thus, it makes sense to evaluate this relationship from different perspectives, including intelligence, economics, defense, and sociological. Those aspects are part of this much-needed assessment because US-Saudi relations are based not only on shared strategic, security, and economic interests but also on what happens within Saudi Arabia and the entire Middle East.

In this context, it is fair to state that the pinnacle of US-Saudi relations happened during the era of the late king Fahd and Ronald Reagan. During that period, US-Saudi relations enjoyed tremendous success and displayed a strong partnership. The reason is that, during the 1980s, the desert kingdom aligned its interests with those of the United States. King Fahd saw the opportunity to divert a portion of his country's unlimited financial resources toward supporting the United States' effort in defeating communism, and he seized it. However, King Fahd's death might have changed the trajectory of US-Saudi relations. There is a consensus among the intelligence, foreign policy, and business communities that the basis of US-Saudi relations is oil for security. Both parties benefit from each other because, in the past, neither party had an alternative to forgo the relationship with the other. Today, that picture has changed, and voices in both Washington and Riyadh are loudly suggesting other options. Because of this emerging thinking, I find it helpful to give readers a glance into how to sustain the relationship. Before doing so, I put my perspective within the context of domestic changes in both countries, the US and Saudi Arabia.

Intelligence Aspect

From an intelligence perspective, questions are already emerging in Washington whether the impulsive crown prince and de facto leader, MbS, is capable of managing a cooperative relationship with the US intelligence community similar to the one enjoyed by the now-deposed former crown prince Mohamed bin Nayef (MbN). This is crucial because the Saudis consider religion one of the pillars of their relations with the US. Yet, Saudi Wahhabism is now under duress from being under the microscope. While the Al-Saud family draws *some* of its power from the religious establishment's unquestionable support, the United States' inability to challenge Saudi Arabia after 9/11 supports my argument. Further, the Al-Saud removed MbN from power. MbN had close ties with the US ███████████████████████████████, MbS's rise to power may convince Russia and China to woo him into their folds, given his youth and inexperience. Consider that, on October 6, 2017, King Salman made a historic trip to Russia, the first ever for a sitting Saudi monarch. Riyadh thought, at that time, that the desert kingdom should reconsider its options given the ongoing civil war in Syria. King Salman's trip to Moscow came on the heels of the United States' decision to end a military-aid program for the Syrian rebels. However, Saudi Arabia sees it otherwise. It perceives it in terms of the US losing its influence in the region. Riyadh's interests are better served if Saudi Arabia changes its stance immediately: "The Saudis now realize that the Russians could be the only party that can settle the Syria conflict,"[119] argues Mustafa Alani, head of the Defense and Security Department at the Gulf Research Center in Dubai. I believe that Russia and China's success in influencing Saudi Arabia's direction will deal a blow to the already declining US influence in the greater Middle East. More and more, Saudi Arabia is thinking in terms of its geopolitical calculations in the region and beyond as Russia and China grow their economic and political presence in a fast-changing Middle East.

Under no circumstances do I suggest that the relationship between the US and Saudi Arabia will end. To the contrary, this relationship will continue for decades regardless of any diminution given the role Saudi Arabia plays in not only the Middle East and the Muslim world but also worldwide. The 9/11 attacks did not fundamentally change the special relationship between Washington and Riyadh. One hates to imagine a calamity that would. Indeed, the 9/11 attacks brought both countries to share intelligence and begin joint counterterrorism ventures. Undoubtedly, almost a decade after the 9/11 attacks, terrorism still challenges Saudi Arabia and the United States. The Saudis fear that large numbers of disenchanted, homegrown Saudis will become active in Syria, Iraq, and other places. By contrast, US intelligence and law enforcement communities struggle to understand how attackers become "radicalized" and how to contain radicalization within US borders. Two recent terror attacks in New York City demonstrate the threat. The radicalized 29-year-old Sayfullo Saipov, from Uzbekistan, conducted a terror attack on November 1, 2017. Twenty-seven-year-old Akayed Ullah from Bangladesh conducted a terrorist attack on December 11, 2017. Both terrorists pledged their allegiance to ISIS beforehand. Fortunately, ███ are still working closely with Saudi Arabia's counterterrorism efforts, especially the latter's rehabilitation program, which has been introduced into Saudi prisons.[120] Keep in mind that no one knows of the ultimate success or failure of this program since the Saudis are so secretive about it.

Defense and Counterterrorism

Security remains one of the pillars of US-Saudi relations. Sales of American weapons to the desert kingdom have been the relationship's lifeline. The United States also provides security for the Persian Gulf given the sensitive economic role it plays as the transportation hub for oil exports to world markets. The United States' interest in the security of the Gulf goes back decades. However, maritime security, though now under the US security umbrella, was managed before 1979 by Iran, under the shah, and Saudi Arabia. However, since the ouster of the shah by the Iranian revolution of 1979, Saudi Arabia has been the only US ally managing that part of the Middle East for almost three decades.

As stated previously, the two main elements of the US-Saudi relations are oil and security. It is worth noting that the Soviets' invasion of Afghanistan in the 1980s and the first Gulf War in 1991 cemented the defense relationship between the US and Saudi Arabia. While that cooperation still exists today, Saudi Arabia requested the removal of US troops from Saudi soil. The presence of the American soldiers triggered terrorist activities inside the KSA that eventually propagated beyond its borders. The Council on Foreign Relations notes, "The presence of U.S. soldiers in the kingdom drew ire from conservatives there and reinforced Wahhabi arguments that the Saudi elite was too accommodating to Western and non-Muslim interests."[121]

Presently, questions are emerging in Washington and other Western capitals concerning how the Saudis are using American weapons in Yemen. Use of those weapons has caused major destruction and famine on an unprecedented scale. Some of the European countries, Great Britain included, have banned the sale of their weapons—in words though not in deeds—to the Saudis. Lawmakers within the halls of the US congress are calling for Saudi Arabia to halt its barbaric atrocities against the Yemeni civilians. Because of those atrocities, the Obama administration suspended the sale of precision-guided missiles to Saudi Arabia. The suspension not only underlines tensions between Obama and the Saudi leadership, but also underscores the shifting priorities of US-Saudi relations. As of this writing, President Trump is trying to reverse former president Obama's decision by prompting a congressional debate over the sale of those weapons.

Economic Aspect

Economically, for the US, access to cheap oil from Saudi Arabia remains the most important part of the relationship. However, falling oil prices on the global market are changing the calculus for Saudi Arabia more so than it is for the United States. That said, the desert kingdom is now facing major economic challenges of a magnitude the country has never faced before. Since 2014, falling oil prices have changed the economic outlook for not only Saudi Arabia and other OPEC members but also for consumers, including the United States. My focus, however, remains how Saudi Arabia intends to engage this new reality when its economy—and survival, for that matter—depends greatly on two vital elements: the United States and oil wealth. OPEC's policy not to cut production aims to eliminate competition that includes America's shale oil industry. However, another reality looms large: China's appetite for Middle East oil. China's thirst for oil—especially its recent demand for *Iranian oil*—led Saudi Arabia to undermine Iran. The journalist Aizhu reports that Chinese firms estimate that China loaded between 3 to 4 million barrels of Iranian oil each quarter in 2017 over 2016.[122] Similarly, other energy analyses suggest that China is reducing its imports from Saudi Arabia due to the latter's decision to cut production. Beijing is already increasing its oil imports from Iran to compensate for the difference. According to Altaqi, of the Orient Research Center, India and South Korea are emerging as the second and third-biggest buyers of Iranian oil.[123]

Given those economic developments, I can see why Saudi Arabia is pivoting toward Asia: the next economic boom is already happening there. The only question is whether it is *big enough* to prompt Riyadh to process payments for oil shipments to China in the Chinese currency, the Yuan, instead of the US dollar. The Yuan is already circulating as a global currency since it joined the International Monetary Fund's (IMF) basket of reserve currencies, in 2016. Should Saudi Arabia proceed to accept payments in the Chinese currency, I wonder whether and how that choice may affect US-Saudi relations.

The world has changed, and the US-Saudi relationship has to change with it. The post-Cold War era compels Saudi Arabia to change its economic priorities. It simply cannot rely, as it once did, on supplying the US with oil. Could that explain why King Salman traveled to China? I believe so. The Saudi monarch signaled the shift of the Saudi economic outlook from the United States to Asia, mainly China. That is the correct decision if the desert kingdom seeks, as it should, to compete by *diversifying* its economy. Now countries like China, which import oil from Saudi Arabia, have other options available: Iran, for instance. Even the United States has options to depend not *solely* on oil imports from Saudi Arabia. The United States has plenty of oil under its own soil to satisfy domestic consumption. According to the Institute for Energy Research's calculations, some estimates suggest that the United States sits on 1.442 trillion barrels of recoverable deposits.[124] Similarly, researchers state that the sprawling Permian Basin in West Texas could allow oil producers using advanced drilling rigs and fracking to extract up to 70 billion barrels of crude.[125] That said, I caution that estimations can sometimes be politically and economically manipulated. Suffice it to state that it benefits Saudi Arabia that the United States still depends on the desert kingdom for its energy needs.

Today, the economic reality is gloomier for Saudi Arabia than for the United States. The Saudi population is growing at a faster rate, which leads to demands that the Saudi government cannot accommodate. As of this writing, the current population of Saudi Arabia is about 33 million, including migrant workers, according to the latest United Nations' estimates. Even more concerning is that a fast-growing population and shrinking reserves can be a volatile combination, especially if a large segment of that population is unemployed. Worse yet, falling oil prices are forcing Saudi Arabia to face the reality: its oil will not last forever. I argue that rising unemployment among the Saudi youth, the lavish lifestyle of the Al-Saud family, and shrinking reserves have combined for a disaster in the making. When considering all those factors, in addition to some 60 percent of the population under the age of 25, I argue that demonstrations are on the horizon. The unrest could shake the Saudi government at its core.

US-Saudi relations have reached a turning point. Asia's growing oil demands seem to have convinced the Saudis to pivot away from the United States (while maintaining security arrangements with Washington) and preposition itself for the impending economic change. Unfortunately, for Saudi Arabia, Iran and Qatar have already embarked on that train and intend to benefit from major economic ventures with China, India, and South Korea. Maryelle Demongeot, deputy Singapore bureau chief at Energy Intelligence, writes, "The Beijing-based China Energy Research Society sees Chinese oil demand growth between 2016 and 2020 even lower than CNPC's Wang at just 2% a year, falling to an annual 0.8% over the next decade and peaking sometime between 2025 and 2030 at around 13.2 million b/d, up from 10.78 million b/d in 2015."[126]

Given those developments, it makes economic sense for Saudi Arabia to forgo its energy ties to the United States and forge new partnerships with Japan, China, and others. Bronson writes, "Between July 2003 and January 2004 Crown Prince Abdullah supported the diversification of Saudi Arabia's economy away from the United States. American oil companies lost lucrative Saudi gas contracts to Lukoil, Sinopec, and Total, major Russian, Chinese, and French companies respectively."[127] I am convinced that the emergence of an "axis of oil," which consists of Russia (a major producer), China (a growing consumer) and Iran (a major producer), will compel the desert kingdom to reconsider its geopolitical and economic options. One of those options is whether Saudi Arabia should break with the United States, economically speaking, when considering China's biggest suppliers are Russia and Saudi Arabia. As China's demand continues to grow, its dependence on Saudi oil shipments is only going to increase. That increased demand comes on the heels of Saudi Aramco's preparation to float on international capital markets. In that case, Beijing may have the perfect opportunity to buy the loyalties of the world's largest oil exporter.[128]

Social Aspect

Socially, US-Saudi relations ultimately affect what is taking place within the desert kingdom. Current social realities look bad for Saudi Arabia. If left unsolved, rising unemployment among the Saudi youth will eventually lead to social unrest. A majority of the Saudi population is under the age of 30, with neither jobs nor economic prospects. The young generation is questioning how the Al-Saudi family leads a lavish lifestyle while poverty is on the rise, necessities are diminishing, job training is lagging, and economic opportunities are scarce. The Saudi population also wonders why the United States is encouraging the sale of more American weapons to Saudi Arabia. Those transactions come at the expense of the Saudi economic infrastructure, education reforms, and other aspects of improving the living conditions of average Saudis.

Bearing that in mind, I believe that both Riyadh and Washington are thinking separately about the available strategic choices. On the one hand, Saudi Arabia has already hinted at pivoting toward Asia. On the other hand, the United States wonders how to proceed given the current administration's lack of vision, clarity, and direction regarding its foreign policy toward not only Saudi Arabia but also the greater Middle East. Regrettably, the Trump administration has no policy in the first place; thus, it is unrealistic to talk about the future of a partnership.

Within this setting, the social element that affects US-Saudi relations will come to the fore, thus leading to the question whether the United States needs to rethink the future of the relationship. Consider the risk involved if Washington decides to scale back its relationship with the Saudis. The Saudi monarchy will lean on its religious establishment for domestic support, resulting in the reemergence of hardliners and unprecedented support of terrorism.

As of this writing, I believe US-Saudi relations will survive for some time to come, assuming the desert kingdom remains stable in the near future. However, MbS's erratic policies, inexperience, and impulsiveness have brought that stability into question. The arrest and detention of other royal princes also casts doubt on MbS's leadership. That ill-conceived decision sets the stage for what lies ahead if MbS succeeds his ailing father to the throne after King Salman's demise. Again, the pages of history recall a similar scenario, namely, King Faisal's assassination, in 1975.

President Trump's administration is chaotic, makes erratic decisions, and experiences a lot of turnover. The political changes coming to the Middle East will not be to the liking of both Saudi Arabia and the United States. It looks to me as though Russia, Iran, and Turkey are already setting the political agenda for the region. In addition, China is increasing its economic ventures in the Middle East, forging new economic partnerships, and expanding its global reach. Those dynamics give a strong signal that the United States' hegemonic days and years are numbered.

What Lies Ahead?

Some apologists argue that nothing is wrong with US-Saudi relations. Those same apologists say that everything is working in harmony, and great things should emerge from this everlasting relationship. I agree that US-Saudi relations will survive the next decade or so, but they will eventually collapse. That is not because Washington wants such an outcome. Rather, several issues will cause the collapse. Those issues include the desert kingdom's demise from within. Specifically, royal infighting will lead to factions based on bloodline that undermine each other. Other countries like Iran, Kazakhstan, and Russia may meet the demands of the global markets that Saudi Arabia once provided. Saudi society, particularly the young, will feel the loss of oil revenue. Eventually, the Saudi population will wake up to the reality that the Al-Saud monarchy has all along used religion to justify its monopoly on the country's resources to fund its lavish lifestyle. Eventually, the marginalized, the minorities, the disenchanted youth, and the forgotten will demonstrate in the streets. They will force the

Saudi government to either meet their demands or face the consequences of civil disobedience and social unrest.

US-Saudi relations survived the 9/11 attacks. But the families of the 3,000 Americans who died have not received justice on behalf of their deceased loved ones. The American people are confused and perplexed about a tweeting president who has no clue how the Saudis have played him, wanting him to engage Iran militarily on the Saudis' behalf, sacrificing American soldiers for a few billion dollars in return. America's moral standing has succumbed to dark money, power, and corruption. Those vices have led Americans to turn a blind eye to Al-Saud's culture of bribery, its abysmal human rights record, and its financial support of fundamentalist Islamic groups that have been directly linked to international acts of terror. Those acts of terror include some against the United States, as Robert Bear, retired CIA officer, argues in his book *Sleeping with the Devil: How Washington Sold our Soul for Saudi Crude.* Yes, US-Saudi relations will survive *but only because* officials in Washington put self-interest, ego, and self-worth before the welfare of the United States. US-Saudi relations will survive *but only because* America has corrupt politicians in power who lack the ethical resolve to speak the truth. However, it is my duty to inform readers in America and throughout the world that the US-Saudi relationship will not last forever. Saudi society and the political landscape of the Middle East are changing by the hour, as Saudi Arabia lags behind while mistakenly thinking it is leading.

A new thinking is emerging in both Saudi Arabia and the United States. This new thinking begins with both subjects and citizens, who all see reality for what it is and seek a path forward to meet their needs and achieve their dreams. Both the American and the Saudi people know that their leaders must wake up, and they must reassess the relationship between the two powers. Even long-lasting relationships eventually end, and everyone must be ready when that day comes.

CHAPTER V

Iran-Saudi Arabia Rivalry

Introduction

Addressing the various religious interpretations that led to the Shia'-Sunni separation would be a full-length text. This section therefore focuses only on the main cause for the split between those two Islamic sects. The split occurred soon after the death of Prophet Muhammed, in 632. While the split was originally over who would succeed the prophet Muhammad, the present-day rivalry between Sunni-dominant Saudi Arabia and Shiite-dominant Iran is *partially* over geopolitics, nationalism, and ideology. Although acquiring religious leadership is *part* of the issue, it is not the entire issue. One should recognize that politics also drives the rivalry.

This chapter details the core issues of the rivalry and its ramifications. My objective is to not only identify important questions but also provide answers that place both Saudi Arabia and the Middle East within the context of the Saudi-Iran rivalry.

This section begins by briefly addressing the religious aspect of the rivalry, to understand why it exists. Then the section examines the Saudi-Iran rivalry through economic, geopolitical, and ideological lenses. This chapter concludes with my perspective on how this rivalry will continue to be problematic and precarious in the coming decades. The problems will be made manifest as Saudi Arabia's leadership submits to the truth of a domestic and regional economic, geopolitical, and social shifts beyond its control.

Religious Rivalry: Saudi-Iran Debate and Divide

The split between Shi'a and Sunnis originates mainly from the question of the rightful successor to Prophet Muhammed. At the time of the prophet's death, his followers suggested that the Muslim community should choose his successor. Others, mainly minority Shi'a, wanted the successor to be a member of the prophet's family, notes Gregory Gause, professor of Middle East politics at the University of Vermont, as reported by National Public Radio.[129] The consensus was that Ali, Muhammed's son-in-law, fit this profile given that he was married to the prophet's daughter, Fatimah. The Sunnis strongly advocated for the elite of the community to choose the prophet's successor, but their wishes were unrealized. Subsequent divisions over leadership contributed to the political split between Sunnis and Shi'ites. The division persists to this day. Amid this chaos, Ali was chosen as Prophet Muhammed's successor, the fourth caliph. Ali's two predecessors were assassinated. Unfortunately, a battle near the city of Kufa claimed the life of Ali himself, in 661. As an aside, Kufa is located in the south of modern-day Iraq and served as the center of Arab culture and learning from the 8th through the 10th centuries. Ali's death further deepened the division within the Muslim community, splitting it into two branches. Regrettably, those branches will never reunite. With Ali's death, his son Hussein took the lead and continued the war, sending a message of rejection to the new caliph at that time. However, the caliph's army massacred Hussein and his family.[130]

The preceding brief historical account highlights the complexities surrounding the Shi'a-Sunni divide. In the last few centuries, the divide has manifested itself beyond the religious realm. Further, information about this ongoing split reminds us of how daunting a task it is to resolve a 1400-year-old-struggle. That is why I do not subscribe to the idea that Saudi Arabia and Iran can or *ever will* get along. The resentment and mistrust between these two countries runs deep.

Further, discussing the religious aspect brings to the fore the history from which Saudi Arabia circulates its baseless claim that Iran desires to dominate the Muslim world. Statistically speaking, the numbers oppose Saudi Arabia's claim. Iran has neither the interest nor the ability to get that leadership over the Muslim world. Iran realizes that its minority Shia population of about 170 million worldwide cannot control a Muslim population of 1.6 billion and that Sunni Muslims will not allow it.[131] In my opinion, Saudi Arabia's claim that "Iran wants to take over the Muslim world" is a tactic the desert kingdom uses to mask its economic and social failures and hide behind the facade of Muslim unity and other slogans. To illustrate, some Muslim countries, including Saudi Arabia, use the Arab-Israeli conflict to demonstrate their concern. In reality, those same Arab/Muslim countries "do not give a hoot" about Palestine or the Arab-Israeli conflict. They use the conflict to mask their inadequate leadership and failed economic, educational, and social policies. Saudi Arabia bases its domestic and foreign policies on the perceived needs and whims of the Al-Saud monarchy. In doing so, it is no different from several other Muslim countries that ignore the wishes and demands of their own citizens, the Palestinian people, and the Muslim world writ large.

Neither is the Palestine Liberation Organization (PLO) leadership interested in peace with Israel. If it were, it would have accepted the Oslo Accord—in my opinion, the best offer ever. When former PLO leader Yasser Arafat passed away, it was revealed that funds were transferred from a Swiss bank account to his wife's private account in Paris, France.[132] The PLO wants to continue the flow of financial assistance from other countries to support the "cause." Yet, that financial support ends up in private Swiss bank accounts, and the Palestinian people do not see a dime of it. It has been that way for decades and will continue to be.

Undoubtedly, the religious aspect of the split between Shi'a and Sunnis affects many Muslim communities' peaceful coexistence. One finds examples in Pakistan, Iraq, India, Saudi Arabia, and Yemen. As previously discussed, the history of the Shi'a-Sunni split dates back to the earliest years of Islam. However, Saudi Arabia's present-day promotion of its Wahhabist ideology aggravates the rivalry today. That ideology comes with declarations of anti-Shiite dogma and the designation of Shia followers as heretics. Innocent people who have nothing to do with the division also are caught up in it. For example, witness what is happening in communities within Iraq and Syria. Even Christians, who have nothing to do with the split, find themselves targeted by Sunnis and Shiites, who try to "cleanse and purify" the area under their respective control.

The religious rivalry between Saudi Arabia and Iran is centuries old. Saudi Arabia is noticing the decline of its influence in the Muslim world, though not entirely. Two of Islam's holy sites, Mecca and Medina, which are part of the pilgrimage, are located in Saudi Arabia. Thus, some influence remains. Speaking of pilgrimage, debates in some Muslim communities are ongoing regarding what gives Saudi Arabia the right, the authority to decide and control the process of pilgrimage, one of the five pillars of Islam. It is as though the desert kingdom politicizes the pilgrimage to gain an unfair advantage. To illustrate, Finn writes, "Qatar has accused Saudi Arabia, which hosts and supervises the haj, of deliberately making it hard for its pilgrims to obtain permits to go to Mecca. Saudi Arabia says Qatar is seeking to politicize the ritual for diplomatic gains."[133] However, some argue to the contrary. For instance, Saad Alsubaie, International Security Fellow at the National Council on US-Arab Relations in Washington DC, suggests that Qatar and Syria are the ones politicizing the pilgrimage. That is far from the truth since voices like those of Alsubaie try to portray Saudi Arabia as the victim. Alsubaie writes, "This year (2017), Syria and Qatar are experiencing chaotic political crises; they are in desperate need of a political opportunity to relieve their isolation. Therefore, it is not surprising that they have seized the moment and called for the internationalization of Hajj. Both governments have accused Saudi Arabia of placing restrictions on their pilgrims despite the fact that the Saudi government is hosting their pilgrims on its own expenses."[134] Consider the irony of who reported Alsubaie's statement. The story comes from Al-Arabiya News Network, which was launched in 2003 in Dubai, United Arab Emirates. It is owned by a Saudi broadcaster, the Middle East Broadcasting Center (MBC). Readers can draw their own conclusions.

As the geopolitical landscape in the Middle East is shifting against Saudi Arabia, the desert kingdom is attempting to salvage its declining regional leadership. Religion plays a pivotal role, especially among united groups, in moving various agendas forward. By claiming that Iran wants to dominate the Muslim world, Saudi Arabia wagers that Sunni Muslims will sympathize with its claim, support its concerns, and heed its warnings. The Saudis further push the religious rivalry to mask their economic failures, specifically, a double-digit unemployment rate. They also attempt to distract from the failed policies of Mohammed Bin Salman (MbS), the de facto leader, their disgruntled youth, who are about to explode, and the oppression of its Shi'a minority.

To reiterate, Saudi Arabia uses Islam to its benefit and is indifferent toward Muslim unity or any other bravado that gives a false sense of hope in the Muslim world. Under no circumstances am I suggesting that Iran is the victim here. It is not! Iran's aspirations, religious and otherwise, go beyond the borders of the Islamic republic. Those aspirations encompass the greater Middle East and aim to build a Shi'a crescent that extends from Tehran to the Mediterranean Sea. However, to claim that Iran wants to take over the Muslim world, as Saudi Arabia does, is farfetched by any stretch of the imagination.

Economic Rivalry

Iran and Saudi Arabia do not see eye to eye on a host of issues—that is no secret. However, the two countries sometimes agree on oil cartel policies set by the Organization of the Petroleum Exporting Countries (OPEC). Both rivals are vital members. Yet, the animosity between Iran and Saudi Arabia is a persistent feature of Middle Eastern geopolitics. Certain characteristics define how one country gains an advantage over another. For instance, the population of Iran is far larger than that of Saudi

Arabia. On the other hand, the desert kingdom sits on massive oil reserves in addition to housing the two holiest sites in the Muslim world. Why is this important? The answer lies in defining the economic parameters within which each country draws its strength.

Economically speaking, oil lies at the heart of the contention between Iran and Saudi Arabia. Both countries are members of OPEC. However, due to its massive reserves, Saudi Arabia holds sway over other OPEC members. The Saudis expect other OPEC members to fall in line with its dictates; for the last 3 or 4 decades, most countries did. However, the reality is different today, especially after Iran's agreement with the West over its nuclear program. With the nuclear agreement comes the lifting of sanctions on Iran, which allows Iran to sell its oil on the global market. Consequently, Iran's oil for sale on the international market depresses prices and lessens Saudi Arabia's oil revenues. Worse yet for Saudi Arabia is that other countries, including France's oil giant, Total, and China have signed major energy deals with Iran. Similarly, Norway and Denmark have expressed interest in undertaking economic ventures with Iran. Those unexpected outcomes concern Saudi Arabia greatly as it seeks ways to undermine Iran in any way it can.[135]

Note that both Saudi Arabia and Iran continue to engage China economically by signing major energy contracts with Beijing. Those agreements highlight the ongoing competition between the two Muslim nations. Yet, the existing rivalry between Saudi Arabia and Iran is not only economically based but also driven by geopolitics, security, and nationalism.

One notices major differences when comparing Iran's and Saudi Arabia's capabilities. Those differences in capabilities are possibly what prevent Iran and Saudi Arabia from warring with one another. Militarily, Iran is in a stronger position than Saudi Arabia. That strength begins with the number of possible recruits for the armed forces. Iran has a population of about 80 million while Saudi Arabia's population is only 19 million when one excludes the 30 percent of expatriates living in the desert kingdom. Similarly, Saudi Arabia is no match for Iran's substantial infantry capabilities and will be unable to defeat Iran in a conventional war. Granted that Saudi Arabia's purchase of advanced American and

British weapons could tip the balance to its favor in a war, but there are no guarantees of such an outcome.

Iran is far ahead of Saudi Arabia in the areas of education and technology. Saudi leaders realize that the KSA is no military match for Iran, and time is of the essence regarding gaining improved capabilities. The only exception for Saudi Arabia is the intervention of the United States on its behalf. I strongly believe the American people would vehemently object to such a scenario. Saudi Arabia faces a gloomy economic outlook and the resulting geopolitical shifts in the Middle East: the only option left for Riyadh is to divide and rule. Consider the recent resignation of Saad Hariri, the Lebanese prime minister. Whoever thought that a country—in this example, Saudi Arabia—could force a prime minister of another sovereign nation to tender his resignation under questionable circumstances? To shed further light on this intriguing story, no one was waiting for Mr. Hariri when he arrived at the Riyadh airport. This is unusual for an official visit and violates diplomatic protocol. Moreover, Mr. Hariri's personal phone was confiscated. The resignation letter Mr. Hariri submitted contained unfamiliar and unusual language, leading many analysts to speculate that another entity wrote the resignation letter for him and forced him to read it. Nakhoul wrote, "In his speech, Hariri said he feared assassination and accused Iran and Hezbollah of sowing strife in the region. He said the Arab world would 'cut off the hands that wickedly extend to it,' language which one source close to him said was not typical of the Lebanese leader."[136]

The gross domestic product (GDP) fuels the economic rivalry between Saudi Arabia and Iran. As of 2017, Iran's GDP is about $1.6 trillion, according to the International Monetary Fund (IMF). Put those statistics in the context of the Iran-Saudi rivalry, and one concludes that Saudi Arabia has valid concerns about Iran. The data demonstrates how Iran is poised for regional hegemony in the greater Middle East. That reality is shaking the Al-Saud dynasty to its core.

Readers must understand that the best understanding of Middle East geopolitics—particularly the Iran-Saudi rivalry—comes in terms of economic outlook and regional hegemony. Yet, Sunnis and Shi'ites coexisted peacefully for centuries. Both Islamic sects share similar core beliefs and worship the same God.

The bottom line is this: the Iran-Saudi economic rivalry amounts to competition over global energy market supply. With sanctions lifted, Iran is well positioned to expand its economic ties, mainly in the energy sector, with other countries in Europe and Asia. Under the policy of neutrality, China pursues energy trade with both Iran and Saudi Arabia. The Saudi leaders are coming to grips with the reality that Saudi Arabia can no longer use oil as a weapon. Even more concerning for Riyadh is that China, Iran, and India entered into joint economic ventures. As a result, the energy market will undergo changes that put pressure on the already sluggish Saudi economy.

Those developments suggest that the world market has other energy sources that can meet its demands should Saudi Arabia decide to play hardball. Possible suppliers include Iran, the United States, Russia, and Kazakhstan. In fact, Saudi Arabia has recently cut production only to realize that its policy has boomeranged. Iran's increased economic ties with other countries add another dimension to the Saudi-Iran rivalry. It already became clear that countries in the Gulf Cooperation Council (GCC) are benefiting from greater Iranian trade and investments. Qatar is one such beneficiary. It is interesting to speculate on the economy and geopolitics in 2030 after the terms of the nuclear agreement Iran signed with the West in the Joint Comprehensive Plan of Action (JCPOA) expire. Saudi Arabia may be in the dustbin of history by then.

Saudi Arabia's ill-conceived economic and political policies are failing. The considerable cost associated with its ongoing war in Yemen is further contributing to its decline. Saudi Arabia does not know what to do. It failed miserably when it decided to pursue a military misadventure against the Houthis, whom Iran supports. Now, Saudi Arabia is convinced that the time has come for it to enter into some form of political negotiations to end the conflict. Moreover, that will certainly confirm Iran's growing regional hegemony. Welcome to the new geopolitical landscape of the Middle East, in which Iran captains the Middle East political game while the Saudis watch from the sideline.

Geopolitical Rivalry

The shared belief is that the Saudi-Iran rivalry has largely historical and religious origins. However, I argue that the rivalry has evolved into fierce geopolitical competition based on dominance and nationalism despite what one hears from Saudi Arabia that no rivalry exists between the two Muslim countries. It all started in 1979 after the fall of the shah of Iran—Muhammed Reza Pahlavi—followed by Iran's revolution, headed by the late Ruhollah Khomeini. This section details how the growing rivalry between Riyadh and Tehran manifests itself through proxy wars in Yemen, Syria, Pakistan, Lebanon, Afghanistan, and Iraq. Further, it argues that the rivalry will get tenser as Saudi Arabia weakens while Iran's sphere of influence grows. This section concludes that the rivalry will shape the Middle East for decades to come.

Readers must understand the aspects that contribute to the rivalry's evolution, intensifying features, and future trajectories. An assessment of the Middle East today suggests four things. First, Saudi Arabia lacks a strategy in the Middle East. Second, the desert kingdom is lost in the political wilderness. Third, royal infighting over succession mars the country. Fourth, and finally, a sagging economy and high unemployment rate hamper Saudi Arabia because of falling oil prices. Iran takes advantage of the Saudi chaos, which compels me to conclude that Tehran will most likely contribute to this chaos by continuing to support groups like the Houthis in Yemen. Iran is convinced that the policies of the de facto leader, MbS, the young, impulsive crown prince, have failed. Those failures, in turn, suggest not only his inexperience, but also his naivety that military force improves realities on the ground.

The new outlook of the Saudi-Iran rivalry is that it indirectly involves other global powers. China and Russia specifically have increased their presence in the Middle East. The region's geopolitical landscape is influenced by their implemented decisions. For instance, Russia has decided the outcome of the Syrian conflict. China has increased economic ventures with Asia by signing major economic contracts with Iran, Qatar, and Saudi Arabia. As argued in my previous book, *Volatile State: Iran in the Nuclear Age*, China and Russia bet on Iran by supporting it during its nuclear negotiations with major powers (China, Russia, the UK, the US, and France plus Germany, known as the P5+1). China and Russia are not only reaping the benefit for that support, but also deciding on the political and economic trajectories of the Middle East for the near future.

The United States and Saudi Arabia played that role in the recent past—not anymore! The Iran-Saudi Arabia geopolitical rivalry demonstrates that newly emerging players in the Middle East have surpassing influence. Their presence proves that American leadership has declined. Further, Saudi Arabia cannot handle the seismic political shifts in the region alone. Falling oil prices underscore Saudi Arabia's economic vulnerabilities. Finally, MbS's recent detention of royal family members and former government officials under the pretext of fighting corruption is both perplexing and absurd. After detaining the family members, MbS requested that they purchase their freedom. How odd that MbS portrays himself as a champion of change and fiscal responsibility. It was revealed that he was the buyer of (a) the expensive Chateau Louis XIV—with a $300 million price tag, (b) a Leonardo Da Vinci painting (*Salvador del Mundo*) for $450 million—the most expensive art sale in history, and (c) a $500 million yacht from a Russian vodka financier.[137] As argued in previous writings, I believe the socially progressive steps MbS announced are nothing but a smokescreen. The investments listed above cast doubt on his ability to transform Saudi Arabia through his economic "Vision 2030."

Following MbS's campaign of arrests, many countries have questioned both his judgment and leadership ability. Many business entities on both sides of the Atlantic wonder about Saudi Arabia's future stability. I doubt that shrewd investors, who have recently met with MbS in Riyadh behind closed doors, trust him enough when he says he does not intend to carry out more mass-detention "anti-corruption" campaigns against potential rivals in the desert kingdom. Disconcerting is that some detainees, including Major General Ali al-Qahtani, have died while detained. The Saudi government has not explained how they died: "The most dramatic accusation involves Major General Ali al-Qahtani, an aide to a senior Saudi prince seen as a potential rival to the 32-year-old Prince Mohammed, who died in government custody in mid-December. Sources told the newspaper that the general's 'neck was twisted unnaturally as though it had been broken' and that his body had burn marks which appeared to be the result of electric shocks. General Qahtani was taken to hospital in November but was reportedly returned to his interrogation after being seen by doctors. The government has not offered an official explanation for how he died."[138]

Equally important, Saudi Arabia and its allies' (Bahrain, UAE, and Egypt) recent ill-conceived blockade on Qatar supports my argument. Yet, Qatar is prevailing since Qatari leaders withstood Saudi pressure. The unnecessary tensions again proved Saudi Arabia's shortsidedness: It pressured Qatar *unjustly*. Interestingly, Qatar weathered the political and economic storm and came out ahead: its stock market survived, its reserves increased, and most of its entire economic outlook appears promising. The big blow for Saudi Arabia is that Qatar and Iran reestablished full diplomatic ties. The move rattled Riyadh as its pressure on Qatar failed to change the leadership in Doha. What a gift to Iran, I must say! If I were to advise Tehran, I would suggest the following: strengthen economic ties with Qatar. Invite China and Russia to invest in a multilateral venture in the energy sector. Extend opportunities to other Middle Eastern countries, especially Turkey, and ensure that the Houthis take complete control of Yemen. Doing so sends a strong message to Riyadh and the UAE that Qatar can influence the economic and political trajectories in the Middle East and beyond. In addition, as a bonus, India's growing economy benefits from stronger economic ties with both Qatar and Iran.

Let us put these dynamics within the context of the Iran-Saudi Arabia rivalry. Saudi Arabia is in no position to influence political and economic outcomes to its favor. More and more countries now question Riyadh's political fiasco as they assess investing in Saudi Arabia. Those same investors are looking elsewhere for opportunities. Countries like Qatar, Iran, Turkey, and China begin to take precedence.

Yemen is another front that openly exhibits Iran-Saudi Arabia geopolitical rivalry. History has come full circle: in the 1980s, Saudi Arabia engaged a proxy war against Iran in Afghanistan. Saudi Arabia won that round when it supported the Taliban (with US assistance) not only to expel the Soviet Union, but also to instill its Wahhabist ideology in Afghan society. The Taliban became the face of Wahhabism, an ultraconservative form of Sunni Islam based on a twisted interpretation of the *Qur'an* (the religious text of Islam) and the *Sunna* (the body of traditional social and legal practice of the Islamic community). The world witnessed what came after that dark era: oppressing women in the name of Islam, banning education for girls in the name of Islam, forcing men to wear a foot-long beard in the name of Islam, and banning music and entertainment in the name of Islam. Three decades later, Iran and Saudi Arabia face off once again. This time, the confrontation happens in and around Yemen, near the Saudi southern borders. The stakes now are even higher for the Saudis. Pursuant to his arrogance and foreign-policy inexperience, MbS assumed that defeating the Houthis would be easy. He was wrong. How ironic that a decade ago, Saudi Arabia advised the United States to think twice about invading Iraq. Yet, with the ongoing conflict in Yemen, Saudi Arabia demonstrates an astounding failure to follow its own good advice. If nothing else, such widespread myopia explains why Saudi Arabia lags behind as private conversations now underway in many Western capitals focus on Saudi Arabia's future stability and survival.

The United States' invasion of Iraq and Saudi Arabia's invasion of Yemen share a similarity: both countries assumed that military superiority alone could achieve a favorable outcome. That is a shortsided strategy. I argue that the thinking in Riyadh is that Saudi Arabia, equipped with US military hardware, could bulldoze its way into Yemen. That betrays lack of vision, unsound judgment, and arrogance. Interestingly, the Saudi leadership is overselling the outcome of the war (as the United States did in Iraq) while claiming that victory is within reach. Alas, will the Saudis ever learn from history?

My prediction is that, given the current conflict in Yemen, Iran already aims to create another force similar to that of Hezbollah in Lebanon. Doing so provides Tehran with two strong fronts that it can activate at a time of its choosing. However, the Yemeni front will be disastrous for the Al-Saud monarchy. Could that trigger war between Saudi Arabia and Iran? It's possible but unlikely. Both countries have too much to lose. Such military conflict would spill into the West, triggering intervention from major powers. The United States will support its staunch ally, the Saudis, while Russia and China will side with Iran.

As it now stands, Iran, Russia, and Turkey are the key players who decide on the future political landscape of the Middle East. That group most likely will change as the rivalry between Iran and Saudi Arabia intensifies. The intensifying Saudi-Iran rivalry presents major challenges for Europe and the United States, but not as much for China and Russia.

I agree with Helia Ighani, assistant director for Center for Preventive Action, that the rivalry will witness renewed tensions over oil prices, medium- and long-range missiles, and nuclear apparatus.[139] In fact, Saudi Arabia has already expressed an interest in having American companies bid for contracts to build nuclear power plants in the desert kingdom. As for nuclear weapons, Saudi Arabia has made it clear that if Iran acquires the bomb, it will follow suit. After all, the Kingdom of Saudi Arabia

███

in Pakistan.

In my opinion, Iran has the upper hand thus far in its rivalry with Saudi Arabia. Yet, the major fear the Saudis have is Iran's hegemonic expansion on Saudi Arabia's southern borders. I believe that Iran needs to rally Shi'ites in Saudi Arabia's eastern province, in Bahrain (with majority Shi'ites), and in Kuwait if it wants to take the rivalry up another notch. Doing so will certainly change the political calculus for Saudi Arabia.

Ideological Rivalry

It is amazing how a few decades can affect the ideological foundations of an important geostrategic relationship. Consider that Iran and Saudi Arabia served as the "twin pillars" of stability in the Middle East after the United States replaced Great Britain as the region's main global power. When Iran's Islamic Revolution ousted the shah, Reza Pahlavi, in 1979, the region's politics and ideology took on a religious tone and trajectory. After that time, Saudi Arabia made its fear of Iran a priority to address. To counter Tehran's aspirations for exporting its Shi'a ideology, Riyadh invested billions of its petrodollars in the 1980s and 1990s to counter Iran. The Saudi campaign aimed to expand its own Wahhabist ideology across the globe to different countries, including those without a Shi'a population. As a result, Saudi Arabia remains adamant about isolating Iran. Recall my previous assertion that Saudi Arabia uses Islam to gain an advantage. Saudi Arabia promotes Wahhabism by both funding it through petrodollars and declaring that it is the only Muslim country to lead the Islamic Ummah (community). Its declaration is enabled by the two most holy sites in Islam, Mecca and Medina, being located in Saudi Arabia.

However, the mere geographical location of Mecca and Medina makes for a weak argument for Saudi Arabia's supposed religious leadership.

I must highlight the impact that geopolitical events have on this rivalry, specifically, how Saudi Arabia contributes to its own defeat. For instance, consider Riyadh's decision to support the Egyptian dictator Abdel Fattah el-Sisi in his military coup against the Muslim Brotherhood. By doing so, attempting to counter Iran, Riyadh inadvertently aligned itself against mainstream Sunni Muslims and potential allies like Qatar and Turkey. It could be said that Iran took a similar approach. The latter's aggressive intervention in Syria and Iraq alienates potential allies who raise serious concerns about Iran's expansion in the region. As of this writing, Yemen has emerged as a proxy theater in which Saudi Arabia and Iran fight over influence. Saudi Arabia claims that Iran provides the Houthis with missiles that target Riyadh. If the Houthis prevail, and it looks as though they will after the demise of the former Yemeni president, Ali Abdullah Saleh, Saudi Arabia finds itself politically isolated. From the Saudi perspective, Riyadh wants to demonstrate that it has the upper hand in the conflict when it does not. Riyadh wants to claim that it is still the hegemonic regional power when it is not. In my opinion, the conflict in Yemen will continue because Iran and Saudi Arabia each misperceive the other's resources and capabilities. Saudi Arabia wants to prove that it still dominates the Middle East, while Iran wants to cement its presence in the region and beyond.

The ideological rivalry between Iran and Saudi Arabia is part of a complicated multivariable equation. While each country's domestic agenda affects its foreign transactions, more than ever Saudi Arabia is vulnerable. The contributing factors mentioned above appear to impact the desert kingdom's standing in the Middle East and beyond. Most Saudi watchers agree that Iran has more power in the region when compared to Saudi Arabia.

Let us put the Saudi Arabia-Iran rivalry in perspective: the decades-old political order in the Middle East is collapsing. No longer are key players like Saudi Arabia at the helm. The collapse comes from a power vacuum created by the decline of the United States' leadership role in the volatile Middle East. Similarly, domestic factors in both Iran and Saudi Arabia have contributed to, and influenced, the rivalry's trajectory.

Analysis: Saudi Arabia's Perspective

From the Saudi perspective, falling oil prices, rising unemployment, and royal infighting over kinship succession suggest a disaster in the making. Saudi Arabia will be extremely challenged to meet the demands of its youth and simultaneously respond to the other geopolitical shifts in its vicinity. Complicating matters is the Saudi de facto leader, MbS, who, along with the United Arab Emirates (UAE), is engaged in a brutal armed conflict in Yemen that has become a human catastrophe. MbS perceives military conflict(s) as a way to bolster his bona fides, raise his nationalist and international profile, and build support. Now that missiles are starting to descend on Riyadh, Saudi Arabia is calling on its US patron to intervene. Henderson writes, "Tactically, the Saudis and their allies in the United Arab Emirates are bogged down in their mission to reinstate Hadi. Strategically, the missile attack suggests the alliance may be losing—a trend MbS is eager to reverse."[140]

Ideological or not, the danger of the Saudi-Iran rivalry will persist for decades to come; as it intensifies, it will show both countries' inability to manage the crisis. I compare this rivalry to that of the United States and the Soviet Union in terms of a quest for dominance and ideological influence. Yet, the US and the Soviets managed to avoid war, knowing each other's nuclear capabilities and the concomitant capacity for destruction. Of course, my comparison is figurative. Radical elements in both Iran and Saudi Arabia advocate for using nuclear capabilities if available. The desert kingdom has vehemently opposed the West's reaching an agreement with Iran over the latter's nuclear program. The reason is that the Saudis are afraid. Yet, the Saudis have the financial capability to purchase

[141]

As of this writing, Saudi Arabia has requested Pakistan to send ships, aircraft, and troops,[142] according to Reuters. The reason for the request is unknown. In my opinion, Saudi Arabia's request from Pakistan to send military aid shows that the situation in Yemen is not going according to the Saudi plan. Riyadh fears the Shi'a influence hitting closer to home given the recent killing of Saudi troops near its southern borders. I argue that, if Pakistan is careless, it will be pulled into a sectarian regional power struggle between Iran and Saudi Arabia. I am convinced that the Pakistani leadership, including that of its Inter-Services Intelligence (ISI), is weighing how far to go in supporting Saudi Arabia. After all, Pakistan shares a border with Iran and has a sizeable Shi'ite minority, which could create major domestic challenges for Islamabad. If Saudi Arabia gets a bomb from Pakistan, all Iran has to do is to reach out to India to counterbalance those efforts while offering lucrative energy deals, which India needs desperately to fuel its economy. Equally important, Russia and China will most likely support Iran's nuclear ambitions either by acquiring more nuclear power plants or even sharing nuclear technology on a limited basis. Iran has options. Note that Russia has already signed an agreement with Iran to build two new nuclear power plants in Iran's southern city of Bushehr.

While Saudi Arabia makes some defensible claims and has some valid concerns about Iran, Riyadh is manipulating the Muslim world by exaggerating the threat Iran poses. The thinking in Riyadh is that its security arrangements and military support of the United States allow it to do whatever it wants. In a bad-case scenario, the United States will fight on Saudi Arabia's behalf in return for a few billion dollars. Even worse, the election of President Trump has brought a foreign-policy novice to the White House, one who is *amenable to* fighting Saudi Arabia's wars for a few billion dollars. But make no mistake: the Saudis are dead wrong if they take solace from Trump, who conducts foreign policy through tweets and changes his mind on a whim. Counting on Trump to support their regional policies and bellicose rhetoric against Iran will certainly contribute to Saudi Arabia's *own* demise. The effect is that Saudi Arabia weakens itself while strengthening its archenemy Iran.

Some observe that Saudi Arabia fears losing its leadership in the Middle East because Riyadh derives its status from the Muslim/Arab world. However, some Arab/Muslim regimes have collapsed, which has brought civil wars, social chaos, and political and security instability. Egypt, Libya, Tunisia, Syria, Lebanon, and Yemen are all examples. The Muslim countries listed above are Sunni dominant. Although Saudi Arabia is not on that list, it is not sheltered from a youth-led uprising, one that could prove costly to the monarchy. I argue that Riyadh is already lost in the political wilderness, trying to find its way back. An uprising would reveal the resultant breakdown in the ranks. In the meantime, Saudi Arabia will most likely continue weakening itself through its ill-conceived policies and engagements in strategy-absent conflicts. Indeed, Saudi Arabia's fear is most likely a backlash from its youth and the survival of the monarchy. Ross Harrison writes:

> Although Iran clearly represents a threat to Saudi interests, it is the weakness in Saudi Arabia's own Arab ranks, caused by the effects of the Arab Spring and the civil wars, that poses the biggest challenge to Riyadh and the biggest opportunity for Tehran. Ratcheting up hostility towards Iran is likely to prolong these wars, running the risk of further weakening the Arab world, thereby compromising Saudi Arabia's position relative to Iran. The longer the proxy battles between Saudi Arabia and Iran in the region's civil wars continue, the greater the risk that the civil wars could spread to other Arab countries like Jordan and Lebanon, the more splintered the Arab world will likely become, and the more Iran gains in the regional power game.[143]

Let us look forward. As events in the greater Middle East unfold, Saudi Arabia faces major challenges that will further exacerbate the geopolitical, economic, and ideological rivalry with its archenemy Iran. Indeed, assessing the desert kingdom's decline since the death of King Abdullah bin Abdulaziz in 2015 sheds light on two root causes: energy (oil) and chaotic regional policies.

First, falling oil prices certainly contribute to Saudi Arabia's rapid decline, which has tried to undermine US shale oil production as the United States becomes more and more independent of Saudi oil. Another Saudi miscalculation is its refusal to cut oil production, flooding the international market with more oil, which drives down prices. Further, the lifting of sanctions on Iran allows Tehran to sell its oil on the international market, putting more pressure on the Saudis. In turn, the Saudis refuse to cut production. Oil transactions in the energy sector demonstrate the ongoing tensions between Sunnis (primarily in Saudi Arabia) and Shiite (dominant in Iran).[144]

Saudi Arabia's unsound economic policies and desire to drive competition (US shale oil industry) out of business has boomeranged. Its economic outlook is gloomy, and oil prices will *not* return to pre-2014 level. Saudi Arabia is poised to burn through its reserves within a decade, according to the International Monetary Fund (IMF). Saudi leaders must understand that money cannot solve all problems. Nevertheless, the energy sector is one of many elements that define the Saudi-Iran rivalry.

Second, unsound, poorly thought-out policies further contribute to Saudi Arabia's decline. Two illustrations come to mind: Yemen and Syria. In Yemen, the Kingdom of Saudi Arabia misjudged the resistance, strength, and capabilities of the Yemenis. Crown Prince MbS's inexperience, exhibited in the Yemeni theater, is part of the problem. He—and the Saudi government, for that matter—assumed that because of its massive wealth and the availability of US and British weapons, Saudi Arabia would win the conflict. To its vexation, Saudi Arabia cannot declare victory as missile barrages fall on its capital, Riyadh, Houthi rebels kill Saudi soldiers at its southern borders. Unable to control the conflict, Saudi Arabia now bombs hospitals and targets civilians, thinking that it will turn Yemeni against the Shi'ite Houthi rebels. Once again, if the Saudis were to study history, they would learn that engaging in conflicts like the one in Yemen is suicidal. It appears to me that Yemen has become to Saudi Arabia what Vietnam was to the United States. The only option left for Saudi Arabia is either to enter into negotiations with Houthis or withdraw as Gamal Abdel Nasser of Egypt did when he got involved in a guerrilla war in Yemen only to withdraw with a bruised ego.

As the conflict in Yemen persists, Saudi Arabia finds itself in the headlines worldwide for its violations of human rights, creation of famine on an unprecedented scale, and war crime atrocities. Some articles suggest that MbS should be referred to the International Criminal Court (IOC) for the atrocities Saudi forces committed under his orders. In February 2018, the planned three-day visit of the Saudi crown prince, MbS, to London was delayed. Massive demonstrations in London protested the visit—a backlash against the British government's invitation of the Saudi prince, the chief architect of the ongoing Saudi-led bombardment of Yemen. Simultaneously, supporters of Saudi Arabia, including the United States and Great Britain, find themselves in an awkward position. They know that they continue to supply Saudi Arabia with weapons and intelligence that contribute to more, and seemingly unending, civilian deaths. The reputation and credibility of the US and UK worldwide becomes damaged.

In 2018, Saudi Arabia struggles to find an exit from Yemen. The conflict, coupled with low oil prices, is draining the Saudi economy. All Iran needs to do is continue to provide logistical support and weapons to the Houthis to back their hit-and-run attacks near the southern Saudi borders. Interestingly, a large Shi'a majority lives in southeastern Saudi Arabia. If Iran can initiate, and then support, their rebellion, it will mark the beginning of the end of Saudi Arabia as we know it. Guided by the Wahhabist establishment, Saudi Arabia has alienated this segment of the Saudi society, the Shi'a, through decades of harsh oppression and discrimination. Note that the southeastern Saudi region of Al-Ahsa is home not only to the minority Shi'a in Saudi Arabia, but also has Ghawar, the largest conventional oil field in the world. As the Saudi economy declines, the chickens will come home to roost for that injudicious exercise of governmental authority.

Yemen's quagmire exposed the chaotic nature of Saudi Arabia's government. The government malfunctioned by failing to understand the risk involved when engaging in guerrilla warfare. Rigg writes, "The considerable and continuing cost of the Saudi war in Yemen is contributing to the decline of the Saudi economy. A clever Houthi strategy of destabilizing Saudi territories with cross-border military attacks and incursions has added to the pressure on the Saudis to abandon their failed strategy in Yemen, and to seek a negotiated political conclusion to their own self-inflicted military misadventure."[145]

The handwriting is on the wall as the Saudi-Iran rivalry adjusts to new realities. In this new reality, Iran plays a far greater role in the Middle East than Saudi Arabia ever imagined. Not coincidentally, the ill-conceived policies that emanate from Riyadh have failed miserably. Besides policies on oil and Yemen, the blockade on Qatar seems to add more fuel to the fire and destroy any credibility left for the Saudi regime.

A meticulous discussion of the root causes for the blockade would be a great topic for another book. For now, I limit my narrative about this blockade to the context of the Iran-Saudi rivalry. For starters, Saudi Arabia and its allies in the blockade (Egypt, UAE, and Bahrain) claim that Qatar funds terrorists and violent groups affiliated with the Muslim Brotherhood. Qatar does not deny funding the Muslim Brotherhood; the core issue is that Saudi Arabia and its allies fear groups like the Muslim Brotherhood. Saudi Arabia and its allies make the argument that "there is no difference between the Muslim Brotherhood and the more overtly violent extremist groups they face." How ironic for Saudi Arabia to take this position. Consider, for example, WikiLeaks' recent disclosure that Saudi Arabia has been funding both ISIS and radical Sunni groups.

Likewise, Saudi Arabia and its allies claim that Qatar maintains a cordial relationship with Iran. What is wrong with having bilateral relations? Since when can one country (Saudi Arabia, in this case) dictate to another sovereign state (Qatar, in this case) that it have diplomatic and economic relations with it? Saudi Arabia's justification for the blockade demonstrates Riyadh's failure to understand the basic notion of what "diplomatic sovereignty" means.

Even the United States fell into this commixture of ambiguity when President Trump took credit on Twitter for accomplishing the blockade on Qatar. What an odd behavior from a sitting American president. I am convinced that Trump's visit to Saudi Arabia, in May 2017, facilitated this behavior. Apparently, Saudi Arabia and its allies perceived the American president's trip as a green light to punish Qatar. Gordon writes, "In this sense, the Saudi-led move was at once an opportunity for the GCC partners and Egypt to punish their adversaries in Doha, please their allies in Washington, and remove attention from their own shortcomings and challenges."[146]

Against all odds, Qatar is managing well, and the blockade is politically and economically weakening Saudi Arabia more so than it does Qatar. Harrison argues that the blockade was "intended to take Iran down a notch, these actions instead will likely strengthen Tehran's hand. In fact, Iranian policymakers would be forgiven for believing that Saudi Arabia had fallen prey to the judo move by which one's opponents are unwittingly maneuvered to use their own strength to harm themselves."[147] The danger is that, while Saudi Arabia forges ahead in this ambiguous path and proxy conflicts with Iran, it is a forgone conclusion, in my opinion, that the desert kingdom has already undermined and weakened its own regional position while strengthening that of Iran. As a result, Iran perceives a strategic depth that is currently sweeping the region as Tehran exploits the current power vacuum in the Arab world created by division, strife, ethnic tensions, and the economic downturn resulting from falling oil prices. Iran's hardliners are also to gain from the Saudis' ill-conceived policies. Take, for instance, Qasem Soleimani, head of Iran's al-Quds force, who advocates for a confrontational stance toward Saudi Arabia and dilutes voices coming from the foreign ministry and president's office that are less inclined to see the region in zero-sum terms.

The current economic and political landscape of the Middle East suggests that the region has already shifted from an Arab-led system to an Iranian-Turkish system backed by Russia. Thus far, Saudi Arabia's actions in the region have failed to counter Iran's march toward regional hegemony. Tehran's pursuit of this hegemony is facilitated by a sound strategy that combines hard power (intervention in proxy wars) with economic endeavors (economic ventures with Qatar, Turkey, China, France, Germany, Russia, India, and Iraq). Yet, recent protests against Hassan Rouhani's government over the economy and the increased price of necessities hint at more chaos on the horizon.

Some Saudi apologists vociferously argue that reestablishing relations between Iran and Saudi Arabia will bring stability to the region, but their arguments lack depth and understanding of the core issues that define the Iran-Saudi rivalry. The rivalry goes beyond diplomatic representation. Rather, it stems from Saudi Arabia's fear of losing its leadership in the region and the greater Muslim world, for that matter. That leadership now has an expired shelf life.

Let us put the Saudi fear of Iran in perspective. Consider, for instance, Muqtada al-Sadr, a Shi'ite and an anti-American figure who commands a large following among the urban poor of Baghdad and the southern cities. He is visiting the Gulf region as the dispute between Qatar and a Saudi-led bloc intensifies. Once again, the blockade on Qatar highlights the Saudi leadership's lack of understanding of the dynamics of regional and global relations. I have no doubt Riyadh is licking its wounds as the outcome of its policies prove disastrous in Yemen, Syria, Qatar, and other countries. As to Qatar, the country is already forging economic ties with Turkey, Iran, and China, among others.

To change direction, if I may, something triggered my curiosity in the wake of these events: what makes a well-established journalist like Thomas Friedman flip-flop and change his narrative? In one article, he criticizes Saudi Arabia's latest campaign of arrests and detention. But just a few weeks later, he goes to Riyadh to pen an article that praises the crown prince, MbS, and categorizes the de facto leader's dictatorship style as an "Arab Spring" from top to the bottom. Really, Mr. Friedman! While I do not question Friedman's intellectual capacity, I certainly question his judgment given that unexpected turn of events. In fact, others, including Hamid Dabashi, author and Professor of Iranian Studies and Comparative Literature at Columbia University, use harsh words to describe Friedman's argument:

> Imagine the intellectual bankruptcy, try to fathom the moral depravity, of considering what Mohammad bin Salman and Jared Kushner are doing in Saudi Arabia and beyond an "Arab Spring!" Which one is more ignorant: that you have no blasted clue what the Arab Spring was, or your calling the treacherous atrocities of Mohammad bin Salman the Saudi version of Arab Spring? Countless books, piles of learned essays by Arab and non-Arab scholars and critical thinkers have been produced about the minutest aspects of the Arab revolutions. In art, literature, poetry, and scholarship - in scholarly conferences, academic seminars, and learned volumes young and older scholars have done their best to figure out the significance of the Arab Spring and then in comes this propaganda officer and issues page after page of a nonsensical gibberish the likes of which scarce anyone can fathom even in the "post-truth" age of "alternative facts."[148]

More and more Saudi intellectuals and moderate religious leaders are leaving Saudi Arabia for fear of arrests and torture. Their crimes amount to speaking their mind and expressing their serious concerns about where their country is headed. One of these intellectuals is Jamal Khashoggi, a journalist, author, and editor-in-chief of the Al Arab News

Channel. Khashoggi is internationally respected for his contributions to the Al Watan Newspaper, which became a platform for Saudi progressives. Khashoggi expressed his concerns about not only the recent wave of arrests ahead of the crown prince's ascension to the throne, but also Riyadh's implementation of new, extreme policies that encourage citizens to name others to a government blacklist.[149]

The Muslim World's Perspective

The great majority of the 1.8 billion Muslims around the world are Sunnis. Saudi Arabia has an advantage over Iran when it comes to acquiring support from the majority of Muslims. Further, the presence in Saudi Arabia of the two holiest sites in Islam, Mecca and Medina, further strengthens its position within the Muslim world. Yet, Saudi Arabia's leadership is being questioned in many Arab/Muslim capitals not by its governments but by average citizens. However, most financial donations from Saudi Arabia to Muslim governments end up in the private bank accounts of corrupted leaders. For instance, some estimates put former Egyptian president Mubarak's assets during his 30 years in power at more than £3 billion Euros. Other estimates could be as much as £40 billion, according to Philip Sherwell.[150] Of concern, some of the corrupt Arab leaders were supposed to spend the financial assistance on their citizens, infrastructure, education, job training, and so forth. Ask an average Muslim in Cairo, Amman, Baghdad, or Beirut about Saudi Arabia, and one is most likely to hear these and many other negative comments about the desert kingdom: Saudi Arabia uses Islam to its advantage, Saudi Arabia is a puppet of the West, and Saudi Arabia is the most hypocritical and corrupt country in the Muslim world.

Similarly, the Saudi-led coalition against Qatar and Yemen perplexes the Muslim people. Muslims question the motives behind Saudi Arabia's harsh stance on a fellow Muslim country. Muslims argue that Saudi Arabia has double standards. On the one hand, it punishes Muslim countries that disagree with its policies. On the other hand, it bows to its patrons, the United States and Great Britain, when the latter's interests are threatened. Was the United States made aware of Saudi Arabia's intention to blockade

Qatar, or was the US kept in the dark since Riyadh realized how naive President Trump is? Using the US president to deliver the Saudi message to Iran clearly indicated that naivety. Most likely, Washington approved Saudi Arabia's decision to blockade Qatar. Whatever the case may be, the Muslim world is intensely watching how the blockade is brewing in other countries of the Middle East, including the Persian Gulf, a region known for its stability. It also demonstrates how Saudi Arabia is struggling to sustain some sort of Arab unity. One thing is certain: Iran tends to gain from the chaos among Sunnis Arabs in the Persian Gulf.

Conclusion

This chapter helps business leaders, intelligence and global-affairs analysts, and others interested in the Middle East to better understand the parameters within which the Saudi-Iran rivalry plays out. Those parameters are defined through geopolitical and economic dimensions more so than religious factors. The reason is that the Sunnis greatly outnumber Shi'ites. So, it behooves us to put to rest the notion that the rivalry between Iran and Saudi Arabia is religiously based. That is not the case! This outcome leaves us with the following questions: what will become of the Iran-Saudi rivalry? Will it get tenser? Will both countries find common ground on which to agree? Will Iran and Saudi Arabia allow a third party to mediate?

The Iran-Saudi rivalry will most likely intensify. Their proxy conflicts involving Yemen, Syria, Iraq, Libya, Egypt, and Qatar are evidence of those ongoing tensions. The emergence of new players in the Middle East, including Russia and China, will most likely influence the trajectory of this rivalry. That influence manifests itself through economic ventures and political maneuvering. Many Saudi observers will closely watch Saudi Arabia's next move. Questions are already emerging in many Western capitals and among global investors as to the future stability of Saudi Arabia. Moreover, the ambiguity of the Saudi policies under the leadership of MbS, its impulsive de facto crown prince, raises serious questions about his fitness and ability to transform Saudi Arabia from an ultraconservative society to one that marches in lockstep with modern time.

CHAPTER VI

Conclusion

As I conclude this book, I am under no illusion that the future of Saudi Arabia is as obscure as it can be. Forget about the continuing rhetoric, flowery speeches, and empty promises by the de facto crown prince, Mohammed Bin Salman. The desert kingdom's reality suggests otherwise. Before elaborating further, let me clarify that my prediction about the future of Saudi Arabia is based on a host of factors that include my cultural understanding of Saudi Arabia, the persisting economic trend of low oil prices, a high unemployment rate, and geopolitical shifts that render Saudi Arabia a spectator rather than an influencer. Add to that the United States' astounding, overarching lack of advocacy of an *inclusive* international order, an inaction led by President Trump, who personifies Lederer's and Burdick's *Ugly American.*

My purpose herein is to honestly assess and realistically consider the future of Saudi Arabia. However, I do not propose potential solutions because that is the responsibility of the Saudi government and its citizens. My assessment about the future of the desert kingdom simply cuts through the noise and gets to the significant reasons that Saudi Arabia has an unpromising future. I hope that diplomats, business leaders, investors, and analysts from industries interested in Saudi Arabia will heed my warnings and plan accordingly.

My insights focus on three themes: the economy, royal internal infighting over succession, and discontentment of the unemployed Saudi youth. Keep in mind that Saudi Arabia is at the heart of the Middle East—a region known for its shifting loyalties and contradictions—and is already shaken by happenings in neighboring Arab countries. Ongoing demonstrations over the increasing price of necessities in Jordan, Tunisia, Sudan, and Iran send a strong message to the Saudi government that it is only a matter of time before the flames of unrest spread like wildfire within its borders, starting with its restive eastern region.

Let us start with the economic outlook for the kingdom. Crown Prince Mohammed Bin Salman is betting on transforming the Saudi economy from an oil-based one to a diversified economy. He intends to achieve diversification through desert megacities projected in his Vision 2030. Yet, many global investors, especially those who attended the recent theatrical show in Riyadh, wonder about his abilities to achieve those exceedingly ambitious goals. "Is he for real?" asked one of the investors attending the Future Investment Initiative (FII) conference, in Riyadh, in October 2017. Interestingly, the Ritz-Carlton Hotel turned into a detention and torture center a few weeks later when MbS detained royal princes and officials under the pretext of ending corruption. The truth is that those princes and officials criticized MbS's Vision 2030, assessing it to be an unrealistic venture. If I were to advise those investors, I would ask them the following question: does it make economic sense to invest in a country that says one thing and does another? Does it make sense to invest in a country in which its de facto leader rules like a dictator? Once Saudi Arabia descends into chaos, those investors will have to forget about getting a return on their investments.

While I applaud MbS' vision about those megaprojects, I seriously doubt the feasibility of accomplishing such complicated projects. How will Saudi Arabia get the necessary funds, estimated at a half-trillion dollars, to build those megacities? Yet, oil prices are unlikely to go up anytime soon to their pre-2014 levels, and the United States' oil production will most likely surpass that of Saudi Arabia in the next few years, assuming there is a will in Washington for that to happen. Speaking of the US shale oil industry, according to Patti Domm, "The U.S. is the world's third largest oil producer, and its status is growing. Russia is the largest, with about 11 million barrels a day. The U.S. output rivals Saudi Arabia, which has had production of 10.6 million barrels a day."[151] Against this backdrop, it would have made sense for the impulsive prince MbS to take advantage of the international financial expertise that senior princes had acquired over the years. However, desiring to consolidate power, he detained them instead.

Thus far, we are witnessing MbS carelessly spend the country's wealth—the latest purchases he made exceeded $1 billion US dollars. More concerning is the disclosure of recent documents by Craig Caffrey of *Jane's Defense Magazine* in the area of defense and security that show an increase of 17.4% in purchases compared to last year. While MbS seems adamant about his vision and dares anybody in the kingdom to challenge him or point out his flawed strategy, he does not seem to realize that the austerity measures he imposed on the Saudis will eventually boomerang on him and the regime. In my opinion, the Saudi youth will eventually question the practicality of MbS's policies and megaprojects.

That comes on the heels of a sluggish Saudi economy that has deteriorated far more than economists have anticipated. The recent diplomatic row with Canada demonstrates the volatility of the Saudi stock exchange, which has continued its losses for the fourth session in a week in August 2018. This diplomatic row, by the way, is a response to Canada's deep concern over Saudi Arabia's *unjustified* arrest of civil society and its *unjust* detention of female activists. Economic data suggest that the KSA's economy is deteriorating rapidly. If oil prices remain at their current levels, in addition to double-digit unemployment, Saudi Arabia's collapse is inevitable. Further, the Saudi government cannot meet its young citizens' economic demands for jobs as they enter the workforce. Foreign workers in the desert kingdom do the heavy lifting. As to Saudi Arabia's private sector, suffice it to state that it is underdeveloped and unable to overcome the ongoing economic stagnation the country endures. MbS's rosy picture about the future of his country contradicts current realities on the ground. The 80% increase in fuel prices and the imposition of a sales tax of 5% suggest, according to economists, that the poverty level in the oil-rich kingdom will soar to 20%. I doubt that investors are going to gamble on an economy that is spiraling downward. Let us hope that the funds MbS acquired from detained royal princes, as a condition for their freedom, end up in the government coffers and not in a personal account. The famous and brilliant intellectual Ibn Khaldun, an Arab historiographer, historian, and forerunner of the modern disciplines of sociology and demography, warned that if reform did not happen after three family generations of the ruling dynasty, the state would run the risk of collapsing. The Kingdom of Saudi Arabia perfectly fits this description.

Besides poor economic preference, internal challenges within the Kingdom of Saudi Arabia present the greatest challenges. Under no circumstances am I suggesting that Saudi Arabia is going bankrupt. Rather, if low oil prices persist, Saudi Arabia will find it difficult to address the challenges resulting from the loss of oil revenues. I suspect the Al-Saud family has already stashed billions of dollars in foreign banks while average Saudi citizens feel the pinch as commodity prices increase, and sales tax is imposed. The Saudi government needs to come to grips with two things: oil prices are not going back up any time soon, and the geopolitical shift in the Middle East is not playing to its favor[152] That reality needs to be placed within the context of how the decrease in oil revenues impacts the social contract between the Saudi monarchy and its people. This social contract of loyalty for prosperity consists of the Al-Saud purchasing the absolute loyalty of the Saudi people. The bad news is that when the government falls short on delivering the incentives it promised its citizens, the government breaches the contract. That breach of contract leads to social tensions, which become like a pressure cooker that will eventually explode. Once demonstrations erupt, the only option left for the Saudi government to quell them is *violently* to prevent the masses from expressing their frustration: people who criticize the government go to jail. If someone expresses unfavorable opinions about the monarchy, that person disappears. Alas, some of those tactics are already taking place. To get a glimpse into MbS's oppressive governing style, consider the following story: recently, a leading Lebanese talk-show host was summoned to court in Beirut for making a joke at the expense of Crown Prince MbS. The Associated Press reports that "reacting to a clip on a rival network advising bin Salman to swear off fast food for his health, Haddad suggested he should swear off 'fast arrests, fast politics . . . fast military strikes,' instead."[153] When retaliatory arrests start to happen in a civil society like Lebanon's, it sends a chilling message that there will never be freedom of the press, speech, and opinion in the Arab/Muslim world. Sadly, Saudi citizens have been subjected to those cruel, undignified tactics for too long.

In order to divert the attention of the masses from focusing on a failed economy, abuse of power, and drained national resources, the

Saudi government has to create an enemy, a threat of sorts, for its citizens to focus on. Specifically, I refer to the Islamic Republic of Iran and how most of the Saudis talk about Iran more so than they do ISIS, or the high unemployment, or the price increases of commodities, or the royal family's lavish lifestyle. Those facts explain why Saudi Arabia adamantly seeks to steer the United States toward engaging Iran militarily on its behalf. After all, the Saudi leadership realizes President Trump's naiveté. The latter insults countries, but, when abroad or in the presence of those countries' leaders, he switches positions based on personal flattery. The Saudis took advantage of President Trump's ignorance of geopolitics during his first foreign trip overseas, in May 2017. His first stop was to Saudi Arabia, where he delivered what was essentially Saudi Arabia's message to Iran. I will say that the Saudi government has succeeded in manipulating the masses when it rerouted the frustration and anger of the Saudis over austerity measures toward Iran. The Saudi people were probably thinking, "Wow, our government is able to stand up to Iran" or "We are a strong nation!"

Undoubtedly, the future of the Kingdom of Saudi Arabia depends greatly on the United States providing security for the monarchy. Saudi Arabia fully understands that its survival in a tough neighborhood that has no love for, but only animosity toward, the kingdom depends greatly on its ability to keep peace with its neighbors. To navigate those dangerous waters, the Saudi government has to create an enemy, real or perceived (depending on Al-Saud's pick of the day), as part of its survival mechanism. Yet, the objective is to maintain the distraction of a society oblivious to, and obscured from, important societal, governmental, and economic information. The Saudi society is conditioned from cradle to grave to depend on the Saudi government to give it its daily bread in return for absolute loyalty and total obedience. That outcome contributes to a society that is unaware of the danger that lies ahead due to MbS's dictatorial governing style. Even worse is that the president of the United States, Mr. Trump, has neglected to mention the massive scale of unjustified arrests and disappearances of citizens resulting from the Saudi government's recent campaign. Moreover, how could President Trump challenge Saudi Arabia when he insults Muslims and presides over deteriorating race relations within the United States? That is such a great paradox—at a time when humanity looks for justice and social peace. Our longtime ally Saudi Arabia still detains some of the most prominent scholars, thinkers, female activists, and moderate religious leaders. Their crime: they want to raise awareness among Saudis about the dangerous, ill-conceived policies of the current Saudi leadership.

Although I am an optimist, it is clear to me that Saudi Arabia's current dynamics in the Middle East will further contribute to its waning influence and inevitable decline. Undoubtedly, few pundits in energy, finance, and investment sectors may continue to perceive the desert kingdom as relevant and influential. I challenge that assumption and argue that, with MbS at the helm of power, that decline is happening faster and faster due to reckless policies.

I foresee no good outcome for Saudi Arabia. Surely, analysts from the energy, finance, and investment sectors, or even from within the kingdom itself, might continue to perceive Saudi Arabia as relevant and influential. Nothing can be farther from the truth given the impact the drop in oil prices is currently having on the kingdom's economy in addition to the latest wave of unjustified detention of intellectuals, moderate religious leaders, and even members of the royal family. Even with the release, for instance, of Saudi billionaire royal prince Alwaleed bin Talal, MbS's detention campaign has already tarnished his image on the global stage and cast a dark shadow over Saudi Arabia that will last for years to come. During the 2018 World Economic Forum (WEF) in Davos, Switzerland, Saudi Arabia's finance and commerce ministers tried to present Saudi Arabia under positive lights to allure investors. I am sure investors will see through the Saudi rhetoric and avoid falling into the trap. Saudi Arabia's current political and economic influence is declining rapidly. Does it make any sense for investors to bet on a country that is unlikely to change and is on a trajectory toward chaos and instability? Many who applaud, many who support the impulsive crown prince MbS know that he proposes impractical changes. The campaign of arrests is intended to intimidate other royal family members who disagree with his Vision 2030 and consolidate economic and political power. The campaign of detention also sends a message to those who want to join his camp: all they have to do is demonstrate absolute loyalty to MbS. How ironic that something similar is taking place in Washington, DC with President Trump's request for absolute loyalty. Perhaps Trump needs reminding that he is no monarch nor is the United States a monarchy. All the rhetoric and hubris aside, allies and foes alike are perplexed at the conflicting messages Riyadh is sending to the world—thus, the uncertainty about its stability. "These apparently politically motivated arrests are another sign that Mohammad bin Salman has no real interest in improving his country's record on free speech and the rule of law," said Sarah Leah Whitson, Middle East director at Human Rights Watch. "Saudis' alleged efforts to tackle extremism are all for show if all the government does is jail people for their political views."[154]

The Al-Saud family's dark secrets suggest, according to some unsubstantiated reports, that the rise of MbS came right after King Salman ordered his nephew, Crown Prince Mohamed bin Nayef (MbN), to step aside. The reason most likely was MbN's addiction to painkilling drugs. King Salman argues that such an addiction would affect MbN's judgment, problematic since MbN was next in line for the throne. Interestingly, according to those reports, King Salman met alone with MbN when he asked the latter to step down. Similarly, the campaign of kidnapping of Saudi royal princes in Europe who voiced their disagreement with the current Saudi leadership seems further to cast doubt about Saudi Arabia changing any time soon.

Rising tensions among royal family members offer no clarity about what might happen next. The de facto leader, Mohammed Bin Salman (MbS), ascends to power by cutting in line, in front of other royal members (like MbN) who have been waiting for decades. The outcome could be disastrous for the monarchy. As with a regular family, no one wants to be outmaneuvered or pushed aside in favor of another member, especially if the favored member is young, impulsive, inexperienced, and manipulative. In the case of the Al-Saud family with its over 10,000 royal members, I expect that, sooner or later, one of them, through any means, including assassination, will try to "right the wrong" MbS did. After all, the Al-Saud family is too familiar with such an outcome. Recall the assassination of King Faisal, in 1975. My assertion suggests that Mohammed Bin Salman will most likely face rebellion from within the royal family. Those who have been detained and released later will never forget the humiliation they endured and will do their utmost to depose MbS eventually.

This outcome supports the argument some intelligence services like Germany's Federal Intelligence Service (code name CASCOPE) recently made. The agency suggested that, because of its reckless policies, the Kingdom of Saudi Arabia risks becoming a destabilizing force in the Arab world. One does not have to look far to see what is happening in Yemen, Libya, Syria, Iraq, Lebanon, and Egypt. Saudi Arabia's objective is to submit the entire Arab world to its will and impose its leadership on the Muslim world. However, the desert kingdom is neither qualified nor appreciated to claim such a role.

Another issue that looms large and will most likely contribute to the inevitable demise of Saudi Arabia is engaging Iran militarily. While I believe that a military showdown between the two rivals is unlikely, the impulsive MbS thinks that the United States' military backing is grounds for embarking on such a risky proposition and a potential disaster. Doing so will see Saudi Arabia in a series of conflicts, including the possibility of an autonomous Shia region within its eastern border. One considers the steps that separatists in Aden, Yemen, are now engaged in to have Aden secede from the rest of Yemen. If Saudi Arabia is careless, it will only be a matter of time before the Houthis, who control the capital, Sanaa, will support minority Shia in Saudi Arabia's eastern region toward seceding from the desert kingdom.

At the heart of the debate about Saudi Arabia's decline is that Iran's nuclear deal changed the political calculus in the Middle East for everyone; more so for Saudi Arabia than others. Undoubtedly, the Saudi tactics to undermine Iran have failed miserably. The Saudi leadership wonders how Iran sustained itself for the last 37 years despite the West's efforts to undermine it. Ironically, the same Western institutions that zeroed in on Iran turned a blind eye on Saudi Arabia's atrocities and human rights violations. The recent arrests of scholars, female activists, and intellectuals raise serious concerns and compel British lawyers to call for the removal of Saudi Arabia from the United Nations Human Rights Council: "Awda is one of Saudi's most popular Muslim leaders with almost 150 million followers on Twitter. He was recently hospitalised after five months of solitary confinement. It remains unclear why he was arrested. Al Jazeera's Sonia Gallego, reporting from London, said: 'While there may have been quite a lot of drama created by the very high-profile arrests at the Ritz-Carlton Hotel, which was targeting mainly princes, politicians and businessmen, less has been said about these arrests which have caused a lot of concern.'"[155]

Yet, the West continues to shower the Saudis with endless praise and admiration, which does nothing for the Saudis but inflate their egos and infect them with the ancient Greek disease of hubris. I disagree with those who argue that the regional and global prestige the Saudis enjoyed in past decades will endure for future decades. To the contrary, that prestige is fading as the sun sets on the desert kingdom while Iran emerges from the cold, and its star is on the ascendant. Make no mistake: Iran has its own issues to deal with. The latest street demonstrations over price increases of commodities suggest that the lifting of sanctions has not benefited average Iranians. One reason is that the Islamic Revolutionary Guard Corps (IRGC) controls the flow of funding, and corruption is rampant. I am convinced that the religious establishment and hardliners who control the government wonder whether they made a mistake when they reached a deal with the West over Iran's nuclear program. The hardliners have no other excuse, so they blame the West for how things turn out. They probably wish they would have never entered into negotiations in the first place. The Iranian government needs to ensure that the revenues from the lifting of sanctions be used to revamp their economy rather than influence the governments of Syria and Yemen. The proper fiscal focus will reduce unemployment, create job opportunities for Iranians, and, above all, encourage foreign investments. In my opinion, the ongoing demonstrations could turn into demands about what the government intends to do with the revenues now that sanctions have been lifted. The Iranian government will also have to justify why it intends to increase the spending of IRGC forces rather than improve the living conditions of average Iranians. That said, if the Iranian central government delays systematic action, the outcome could be dire.

My prediction is Saudi Arabia's Vision 2030 will fall short because it proposes unrealistic, merely cosmetic reforms. Cosmetic reforms, regardless of their form, shape, and style, tend to fade away. Interestingly, Mohammed Bin Salman is not learning from the lessons of history. Now-embattled Bashar Al-Assad of Syria presented himself as a reformer and played the same role MbS is playing: consolidating power in a dictatorship role.

Look no further than in Yemen where the Saudi Arabia-led campaign demonstrates ugliness and hypocrisy. The Saudi regime claims to embrace the true teachings of Islam. Yet, Islam *does not* call for committing atrocities. As of August 2018, Saudi Arabia is already responsible for the killing of 12,000 Yemenis and the near starvation of 50,000 children, which will eventually lead to their deaths. Seven million people are on the brink of famine in the country, which is in the grips of the largest cholera outbreak in modern history,[156] writes Lydia Smith. Reckon the human tragedies in Yemen, the slaughter of civilians in Syria, and the burning of villages of Rohingya Muslims in Myanmar. Those tragedies convince Muslims worldwide to perceive Saudi Arabia as a country of talks but no deeds, of slogans but no justice, of hypocrisy but no truthfulness. Above all, Saudi Arabia speaks falsehood about being the face of Islam when it is not. It is not enough to dress in white clothing and attend mosques for Friday prayer. It is not enough to build mosques around the world when poverty in Saudi Arabia—and the Muslim world, for that matter—is rampant. It is not enough to pretend to care about Islam and Muslims yet slaughter people by the thousands.[157]

Turmoil in the desert kingdom is *already* underway. The question is whether the Saudi youth will rise up to show the Saudi leadership that its time is up, and change is needed now. Will the Shi'a minority in the eastern region seize the opportunity of chaotic borders to pursue its dream of independence from Riyadh? Will a disgruntled royal family member(s) embark on a plot to assassinate MbS? Screenwriters do not have to imagine a screenplay, characters, plays, drama, and plot twists to produce the best blockbuster of the year, maybe of generations. Rather, they are witnessing a reality unfolding before their eyes that, in the not-too-distant past, would have been unthinkable.

The inevitable demise of the Kingdom of Saudi Arabia is not fiction. It is an emerging reality that requires the undivided attention of diplomats, intelligence officers, foes, investors, weapon dealers, energy analysts, the Chinese, the fundamentalists, and the Shi'a. It requires the undivided attention of the Saudi commoner who wonders whether his life has any meaning, of the Saudi citizen who questions why the Al-Saud have to cater to his needs from cradle to grave, and of the Saudi citizen who realizes the deceit and the bravado shoved down his throat for so long and now grasps the truth that it is not too late to act.

My concluding thought is that when a hardline Islamic entity ends up controlling Saudi Arabia, it will most likely distance itself from the United States in order to acquire some legitimacy in the eyes of the Saudis who want change. At that point, it will probably be time to drop the "Saudi" in Saudi Arabia. The Muslim world will wake up and say, "Good morning, Arabia!"

Endnotes

1   Oualaalou David, "After bluster and bombast, Saudi kingdom reaches out to Iran" *The Waco Tribune-Herald*, August 26, 2017, https://www.wacotrib. com/opinion/columns/board_of_contributors/david-oualaalou-board-of-contributors-after-bluster-and-bombast-saudi/article_6b453d17-769f-52ad-a073-56b19045ee14.html

2   Oualaalou David, "Is Saudi Arabia and Iran on a Collision Course?" *The Huffington Post*, May 10, 2017, http://www.huffingtonpost.com/entry/is-saudi-arabia-and-iran-on-a-collision-course_us_591339aee4b07e366cebb7f1

3   As I argued in a 2017 article, "My sense is that the Desert Kingdom (the royal family) is worried more about its survival and domestic stability. Thus, shifting the conversation and diverting attention could be a good strategy. However, if the people of Riyadh, Jeddah, Dammam, Khobar, and Qatif among others, were to unravel, combined with ongoing issues in the Shi'a eastern province, things could quickly take a different turn. In that case, Iran stands to benefit from a destabilized Saudi Arabia. An unstable Saudi Arabia would pave the way for Iran not only to increase its influence in Iraq, Yemen, and Syria even further than it already has, but also to start working on other Gulf States, including Bahrain and Kuwait. That scenario sends chills down the spines of some observers in Sunni circles. Oualaalou David, "Saudi Arabia Rushes to Mend Relations with Iran" The Huffington Post, August 17, 2017, http://www.huffingtonpost.com/entry/saudi-arabia-rushes-to-mend-relations-with-iran us 59965785e4b03b5e472cee5d7f1

4   Oualaalou David, "Saudi Arabia Rushes to Mend Relations with Iran" The Huffington Post, August 17, 2017 http://www.huffingtonpost.com/entry/saudi-arabia-rushes-to-mend-relations-with-iran us 59965785e4b03b5e472cee5d7f1

5   Vassiliev Alexei, "*The History of Saudi Arabia,*" (New York University Press, New York, 2000), 381.

6   As I argued in August 2017, "Of note for those not near a world map: Shia-majority Iraq lies on the fault line between Shia-dominated Iran and Sunni-ruled Arab Gulf monarchies that include Saudi Arabia." Oualaalou David, "After bluster and bombast, Saudi kingdom reaches out to Iran," *The Waco*

Tribune—Herald, August 27, 2017, http://www.wacotrib.com/opinion/columns/board_of_contributors/david-oualaalou-board-of-contributors-after-bluster-and-bombast-saudi/article_6b453d17-769f-52ad-a073-56b19045ee14.html

7   Shahine Alaa, "Saudi Reserves Dip Below $500 Billion as BofA Sees Headwinds," Bloomberg Markets, May 29, 2017, https://www.bloomberg.com/news/articles/2017-05-28/saudi-net-foreign-assets-dip-below-500-billion-in-april

8   As I wrote in June 2017, "One of the president's worst foreign policy blunders may be born of political convenience or ignorance. Whatever its cause, it is alarming that the president fixes his sights on the Islamic Republic of Iran. Is the president ready to combat Iran on Saudi Arabia's behalf? Most analysis points in that direction, a dangerous path to say the least! Are the statements issued by the Trump camp about cancelling the 2015 nuclear deal the prelude to a much greater plan such as Iranian regime change? Possibly. Trump's limited knowledge of global affairs, Middle Eastern political dynamics, and the shifting regional balance of power suggest that his pursuing regime change will inevitably unleash unrelenting battles between the Shia (Iran) and Sunni (Saudi Arabia) variants of Islam." Oualaalou David, "The Dangerous Possibility of War with Iran," *The Huffington Post*, June 28, 2017, http://www.huffingtonpost.com/entry/the-dangerous-possibility-of-war-with-iran_us_5953ca34e4b0c85b96c65e49

9   Madison Schramm and Ariane M. Tabatabai, "Why Regime Change in Iran Wouldn't Work: Washington Shouldn't Give Up on Diplomacy," *Foreign Policy*, July 20, 2017, https://www.foreignaffairs.com/articles/persian-gulf/2017-07-20/why-regime-change-iran-wouldnt-work

10   Oualaalou David, "Saudis Losing Oil War as Iran Gains Power," *The Huffington Post*, July 14, 2017, http://www.huffingtonpost.com/entry/saudis-losing-oil-war-as-iran-gains-power_us_59690af5e4b022bb9372b15a

11   Blanchard Ben, "China, Saudi Arabia eye $65 billion in deals as king visits," *Reuters*, March 16, 2017, http://www.reuters.com/article/us-saudi-asia-china-idUSKBN16N0G9

12   Mohammad bin Salman bin Abdulaziz Al-Saud, "Vision 2030," Kingdom of Saudi Arabia, http://vision2030.gov.sa/en

13   Chan Minnie, "Chinese drone factory in Saudi Arabia first in Middle East," South China Morning Post, March 26, 2017, http://www.scmp.com/news/china/diplomacy-defence/article/2081869/chinese-drone-factory-saudi-arabia-first-middle-east

14   "China backs Russia after veto of UN demand for end to bombing of Syria's Aleppo," South China Morning Post, October 9, 2016, http://www.scmp.com/news/world/middle-east/article/2026476/china-backs-russia-after-veto-un-demand-end-bombing-syrias

15 Aizhu Chen, "China's Iran oil imports to hit record on new production," Reuters, January 5, 2017, http://www.reuters.com/article/us-china-iran-oil-idUSKBN14P15W

16 Johnson Keith, "China Tops U.S. as Biggest Oil Importer," *Foreign Policy*, May 11, 2015, http://foreignpolicy.com/2015/05/11/china-tops-u-s-as-biggest-oil-importer-middle-east-opec-sloc/

17 Acton Gemma, "Long-term US ally Saudi Arabia is fast becoming firm friends with Russia," *World Economy*, June 2, 2017, https://www.cnbc.com/2017/06/02/long-term-us-ally-saudi-arabia-fast-becoming-firm-friends-with-russia.html

18 I argued in 2018's *Volatile State*, "To Russia's benefit, the ongoing spat between Iran and Saudi Arabia reflects the wider regional conflict between Sunnis and Shi'ites. The cutoff of diplomatic ties between Saudi Arabia (Sunni dominant) and Iran (Shi'a dominant) is not new given how proxy wars across the region expose the issue underlying this religious schism between the two Muslim sects. Given this tumultuous environment, Russia may take revenge for Saudi Arabia supporting the Afghan Mujahedeen against the Soviet invasion, in 1989. It is not the case. The reason is that Russia will want to see how the schism between the two religious rivals plays out. Moscow wants to see if the US will interfere to support its staunch ally, the Saudis, to tilt the cold war to the Saudi's favor. Assuming for a moment that is the case, Moscow already has prepositioned its heavy armaments in Syria and will be in a better position to shift its priorities and support Iran should the need arise. Alas, the outcome could not be more dangerous." Oualaalou David, *"Volatile State: Iran in the Nuclear Age,"* (Indiana University Press, Bloomington, Indiana, 2018)

19 Kosach Grigory, "Possibilities of a Strategic Relationship Between Russia and Saudi Arabia," *Russian International Affairs Council*, August 6, 2016, http://russiancouncil.ru/common/upload/Russia-SaudiArabia-policy-brief-6-en.pdf

20 Chughtai Alia and Saadani Hala, "US-Saudi relations: A timeline," *Aljazeera*, May 20, 2017, http://www.aljazeera.com/indepth/interactive/2017/05/saudi-relations-timeline-170518112421011.html

21 "Yemen conflict: How bad is the humanitarian crisis?" *British Broadcast Corporation* (BBC), March 28, 2017, http://www.bbc.com/news/world-middle-east-34011187

22 Phippen J. Weston, "'Drive Them Out': Trump Addresses Muslim Leaders on Terrorism," *The Atlantic*, May 21, 2017, https://www.theatlantic.com/news/archive/2017/05/trumps-speech-riyadh/527538/

23 Oualaalou David, "Muslims should set record straight about their wildly misunderstood faith," *The Waco Tribune –Herald*, August 7, 2016, http://www.wacotrib.com/opinion/columns/board_of_contributors/david-oualaalou-board-of-contributors-muslims-should-set-record-straight/article_31560cb7-0930-5612-9361-5261e4087b53.html

24 Mohanty, Nirode, "America, Pakistan, and the India Factor," (Palgrave Macmillan, New York, 2013, p.143). (Mohanty, 2013, p. 143)

25 As I argued in May 2017, "Saudi Arabia played its political card well by using President Trump to deliver what is essentially the *kingdom's* message to Iran. What Mr. Trump failed to highlight is the importance of democracy and the rule of law. He failed to stir the Muslim world from its stagnation and its chaotic state of affairs, to engagement with the world. At the same time, are Muslims so naïve to think that conflicts and chaos will resolve themselves? The answer is no. The Muslim community around the world needs to wake up to the reality of how the rest of the world *perceives* it. Imams and religious clerics who take to the platform to deliver fiery sermons pretending to be victims while using the stage to instigate hatred toward others, mainly Jews and Christians, need to reconsider their understanding and interpretation of Islam." Oualaalou David, "Trump's Speech In Riyadh: Political Correctness," *The Huffington Post*, May 30, 2017, http://www.huffingtonpost.com/entry/ trumps-speech-in-riyadh-political-correctness_us_592dc226e4b07c4c7313860f

26 Onis Juan, De, "Faisal's Killer is put to Death," *The New York Times*, June 19, 1975, http://www.nytimes.com/1975/06/19/archives/faisals-killer-is-put-to-death-prince-is-beheaded-before-a-crowd-of.html?mcubz=1

27 As I argued in an article in June 2017, "The elevation of MBS raises serious concerns politically, economically, socially, and religiously. Politically, the main question is what kind of foreign policy the impulsive, inexperienced MBS conduct vis-à-vis Qatar, Syria, and Iran, to name but a few hotspots. One does not have to look far to realize MBS's naiveté in global affairs. Consider, for example, his decision to undertake a military adventure in Yemen. His miscalculation suggests a lack of military and diplomatic experience. Two years after the Desert Kingdom launched its operations in Yemen, it has yet to declare a decisive victory. The underwhelming outcome in Yemen raises serious concerns about how MBS will deal with Iran." Oualaalou David, "The Demise of the Kingdom of Saudi Arabia is Fast Approaching" *The Huffington Post*, June 26, 2017, http://www.huffingtonpost.com/entry/the-demise-of-the-kingdom-of-saudi-arabia-is-fast-approaching_us_595180e0e4b0f078efd9841e

28 Miles Hugh, "Saudi royal calls for regime change in Riyadh," *The Guardian*, September 28, 2015, https://www.theguardian.com/world/2015/sep/28/saudi-royal-calls-regime-change-letters-leadership-king-salman

29 "What is Wahhabism? The reactionary branch of Islam from Saudi Arabia said to be 'the main source of global terrorism," *The Telegraph*, May 19, 2017, http://www.telegraph.co.uk/news/2016/03/29/what-is-wahhabism-the-reactionary-branch-of-islam-said-to-be-the/

30 As I argued in a December 2015 article, "As for the Saudi Kingdom, till it is purged of misguided religious advisers, fanatical Wahhabist ideology and

twisted interpretation of Islam to justify whatever the ends, nothing will change. I do not believe Saudi Arabia or any other country in the region is ready to embrace democracy the way you and I understand, appreciate and practice it." Oualaalou David, "Despite Saudi Women's Historical Vote, Saudi Arabia Still Opposed to Democracy," *The Huffington Post*, December 31, 2015, http://www.huffingtonpost.com/entry/despite-saudi-womens-hist_b_8882020.html

31 Butt Yousaf, "How Saudi Wahhabism Is the Fountainhead of Islamist Terrorism," *The Huffington Post*, (n.d.) http://www.huffingtonpost.com/dr-yousaf-butt-/saudi-wahhabism-islam-terrorism_b_6501916.html

32 "What is Wahhabism? The reactionary branch of Islam from Saudi Arabia said to be 'the main source of global terrorism," *The Telegraph*, May 19, 2017, http://www.telegraph.co.uk/news/2016/03/29/what-is-wahhabism-the-reactionary-branch-of-islam-said-to-be-the/

33 Branson Rachel, "Thicker Than Oil: America's Uneasy Partnership with Saudi Arabia," (Oxford University Press, New York, 2006, p. 169)

34 Hamzei Anahita, "The West and their Tango with Wahhabism: Western Role in Augmenting Extremism," *Khamenei.ir*, June 7, 2017, http://english.khamenei.ir/news/4898/The-West-and-their-Tango-with-Wahhabism-Western-Role-in-Augmenting

35 Al-Semawi Muhammad Ne'ma, "*The Birth of Terrorism in Middle East: Muhammed Bin Abed al-Wahab, Wahabism, and the Alliance with the ibn Saud Tribe*," (Paragon publication, Dearborn, Michigan, 2015 p.5

36 I argued in 2015: "What the general conveniently or ignorantly neglects is that the threat of radical Islam also comes from our supposed ally, Saudi Arabia. How can one forget that out of the 19 hijackers in 9/11 attacks, 15 were from Saudi Arabia? While Iran's involvement (through its proxy Hezbollah) during the 1983 suicide bombings of the US Embassy and Marines barracks in Beirut is well documented, nothing has been more destabilizing than the puritanical Wahhabism ideology that Saudi Arabia has promoted and continues to champion through its petro-dollars. This financial support goes back to the 1970s when the decision in Riyadh was made to get rid of pluralism in Islam and replace it with an anti-western approach to Islam, one that included oppression of women, promotion of an ascetic lifestyle and the spread of religious Madrasas, which educate students on Islam to the calculated exclusion of other critical and enlightening subjects such as math and science." Oualaalou David, "Wake Up America: the Real Threat Beside Iran's Nuclear Deal Is Saudi Arabia's Wahhabism Ideology," *The Huffington Post*, September 8, 2015, http://www.huffingtonpost.com/entry/wake-up-america-the-real-_b_8097038.html

37 The History of Saudi Arabia," *Arabic Islamic Institute*, 2010, http://www.saudiembassy.or.jp/En/SA/History.htm

38 "The History of Saudi Arabia," *Arabic Islamic Institute*, 2010, http://www.saudiembassy.or.jp/En/SA/History.htm

39 Wynbrandt James, *"A Brief History of Saudi Arabia,"* (Facts On File Books, New York, 2004) p. 74

40 Al-Rasheed Madawi, *"History of Saudi Arabia,"* (Cambridge University Press, Cambridge, UK, 2002) (p.15).

41 The History of Saudi Arabia," *Arabic Islamic Institute*, 2010, http://www.saudiembassy.or.jp/En/SA/History.htm

42 "The History of Saudi Arabia," *Arabic Islamic Institute*, 2010, http://www.saudiembassy.or.jp/En/SA/History.htm

43 "Geography," U.S. Library of Congress (no date provided), http://countrystudies.us/saudi-arabia/14.htm

44 "The world FactBook," *Central Intelligence Agency Library*, September 06, 2017, https://www.cia.gov/library/publications/the-world-factbook/geos/sa.html

45 Saudi Arabia Population. (2016, August 06). Retrieved September 11th, 2017, from http://worldpopulationreview.com/countries/saudi-arabia-population/

46 Saudi Arabia Population. (2016, August 06). Retrieved September 11th, 2017, from http://worldpopulationreview.com/countries/saudi-arabia-population/

47 Murphy Caryle, "Saudi Arabia's Youth and the Kingdom's Future," *Wilson Center's Middle East Program*, February 7, 2012, https://www.newsecuritybeat.org/2012/02/saudi-arabias-youth-and-the-kingdoms-future/

48 Chislett David, "What are the oldest languages on earth?" *Taleninstituut Nederland (The Dutch Language Institute)*, November 14, 2016, https://taleninstituut.nl/en/what-are-the-oldest-languages-on-earth/

49 "Culture, Traditions and Art," *Saudi Arabia Cultural Mission*, Retrieved on September 12, 2017, https://sacm.org.au/culture-traditions-and-art/

50 "Culture, Traditions and Art," *Saudi Arabia Cultural Mission*, Retrieved on September 12, 2017, https://sacm.org.au/culture-traditions-and-art/

51 Sedgwick Robert, "Education in Saudi Arabia," *World Education Services*, November 1, 2001, http://wenr.wes.org/2001/11/wenr-nov-dec-2001-education-in-saudi-arabia

52 Mosaad Khadija, "How Will Saudi Arabia Revamp its Education System?" *Fair Observer*, May 25, 2016, https://www.fairobserver.com/region/middle east north africa/will-saudi-arabia-revamp-education-system-11082/

53 Elias Abu Amina, "Protection of non-Muslim houses of worship in Islam," *Faith in Allah*, October 18, 2015, https://abuaminaelias.com/protection-of-non-muslim-houses-of-worship-in-islam/

54 "Saudi Arabia: Religion Textbooks Promote Intolerance," *Human Rights Watch*, September 13, 2017, https://www.hrw.org/news/2017/09/13/saudi-arabia-religion-textbooks-promote-intolerance

55 Yahya Harun, "Islam Encourages Scientific Progress," *The Huffington Post*, April 9, 2013, http://www.huffingtonpost.com/harun-yahya/islam-encourages-scientific-progress b 3047258.html

56 "Basic Law of Governance," *Umm al-Qura Gazette*, March 5, 1992, http://www.wipo.int/edocs/lexdocs/laws/en/sa/sa016en.pdf (p.2)

57 Culbertson Alix, "EU countries selling Millions of pounds of arms to Middle East - especially Saudi Arabia," *Sunday Express*, Mar 3, 2017, http://www.express.co.uk/news/uk/774661/EU-selling-millions-pounds-arms-Middle-East-Saudi-Arabia

58 Riegg Ryan, "WHAT IS SAUDI ARABIA GOING TO DO WITH ITS ARMS BUILDUP?" *Newsweek*, March 17, 2017, http://www.newsweek.com/what-saudi-arabia-going-do-its-arms-buildup-569277

59 "Aramco board to meet in Shanghai as it seeks Chinese investors for IPO," *Reuters*, April 10, 2017, http://www.reuters.com/article/saudi-aramco-board-china/aramco-board-to-meet-in-shanghai-as-it-seeks-chinese-investors-for-ipo-idUSL8N1HH085

60 Riegg Ryan, "WHAT IS SAUDI ARABIA GOING TO DO WITH ITS ARMS BUILDUP?" *Newsweek*, March 17, 2017, http://www.newsweek.com/what-saudi-arabia-going-do-its-arms-buildup-569277

61 Lewis Jeffrey, "Why Did Saudi Arabia Buy Chinese Missiles?" *Foreign Policy*, January 30, 2014, http://foreignpolicy.com/2014/01/30/why-did-saudi-arabia-buy-chinese-missiles/

62 "The Middle East," *The Heritage Foundation*, 2016, http://index.heritage.org/military/2017/assessments/operating-environment/middle-east/#rf42-3599

63 Nazer Fahad, "Will US-Saudi 'special relationship' last?" *Al-monitor*, April 8, 2016, http://www.al-monitor.com/pulse/originals/2016/04/us-saudi-relations.html#ixzz4tLk3Zc00

64 Hinnebuch R., & Ehteshami A, *The Foreign Policies of the Middle East States*, (Lynne Rienner Publishers, INC, Boulder, CO & London, UK, 2014)

65 Partrick Neil, *Saudi Arabian Foreign Policy: Conflict and Cooperation in Uncertain Times*, (I.B. TAURIS, New York, London, 2016)

66 Ottaway David, B., "*The King's Messenger: Prince Bandar Bin Sultan and America's Tangled Relationship with Saudi Arabia*," (Walker & Company, New York, 2008, p. 176)

67 Robert Bear, *Sleeping with the Devil*, (Three Rivers Press; unknown edition, New York, 2004)

68 "After last year's absence, Iran pilgrims flock to Saudi Arabia for Hajj in diplomatic icebreaker," *Hindustan Times*, August 29, 2017, http://www.hindustantimes.com/world-news/after-last-year-s-absence-iran-pilgrims-flock-to-saudi-arabia-for-hajj-in-diplomatic-icebreaker/story-lqcLi021uwleOhTxmiVPQN.html

69 Paton Callum, "HAJJ 'WAR' BETWEEN SAUDI ARABIA AND QATAR LEAVES QATARI PILGRIMS UNABLE TO VISIT ISLAM'S HOLY

SITES," *Newsweek*, August 31, 2017, http://www.newsweek.com/hajj-war-between-saudi-arabia-and-qatar-leaves-qatari-pilgrims-unable-visit-657396

70 Oualaalou David, "*Volatile State: Iran in the Nuclear Age*," (Indiana University Press, Bloomington, Indiana, 2018)

71 Pollack Kenneth, "Fear and Loathing in Saudi Arabia," *Foreign Policy*, January 7, 2016, http://foreignpolicy.com/2016/01/07/fear-and-loathing-in-saudi-arabia/

72 As I expressed in a previous article: "The king's move suggests that the hierarchical structure in the house of Al-Saud, which has been in place for decades, is about to change once and for all. The demotion of Mohamed Bin Nayef (former crown prince and King Salman's nephew) indicates not only the growing power of the young prince MBS (minister of defense, chief of the royal court, chairman of Saudi Aramco supreme council, etc.), but also the oft-unnoticed royal infighting over control of the kingdom. The assassination of King Faisal on March 25, 1975 is a rare example of how such infighting spills over into public view." Oualaalou David, "The Demise of the Kingdom of Saudi Arabia is Fast Approaching" *The Huffington Post*, June 26, 2017, http://www.huffingtonpost.com/entry/the-demise-of-the-kingdom-of-saudi-arabia-is-fast-approaching_us_595180e0e4b0f078efd9841e

73 Castle Stephen and Erdbrink Thomas, "European leaders criticize Trump's Disavowal Iran Deal," *The New York Times*, October 13, 2017, https://www.nytimes.com/2017/10/13/world/europe/trump-iran-nuclear-deal.html

74 Gallarotti Giulio & Al Filali Isam., Yahia, "Soft Power of the Saudi Arabia," *Division II Faculty Publications*, Paper 140., January, 2013,http://wesscholar.wesleyan.edu/div2facpubs/140

75 Mabon Simon, *Saudi Arabia & Iran: Power and Rivalry in the Middle East*, (I. B. Tauris, London, New York, 2015, p. 6)

76 "Rights groups slam Saudi arrests of religious figures," *Aljazeera*, September 15, 2017, http://www.aljazeera.com/news/2017/09/rights-groups-slam-saudi-arrests-religious-figures-170915153115745.html

77 Bradley John R., *Saudi Arabia Exposed: Inside a Kingdom in Crisis*, (Palgrave Macmillan, New York, 2005) (p. 90)

78 Lippman Thomas W., *Saudi Arabia on the Edge: The Uncertain Future of an American Ally*, (Council on Foreign Relations Books (Potomac Books)) Dulles, VA, 2012) (pp. 179-180)

79 Chulov Martin, "Saudi Arabia to allow women to obtain driving licences," *The Guardian*, September 26, 2017, https://www.theguardian.com/world/2017/sep/26/saudi-arabias-king-issues-order-allowing-women-to-drive (Chulov, 2017)

80 Sahih International, "Chapter (2) Surat al-baqarah (The Cow), No date, http://corpus.quran.com/translation.jsp?chapter=2&verse=30

81 Partrick Neil, *Saudi Arabian Foreign Policy: Conflict and Cooperation in Uncertain Times*, (I.B. Tauris, London, New York, 2016) (p. 16-17)

82 "'Secret wife' of late King Fahd of Saudi Arabia wins £20million in damages for 'lavish lifestyle,'" *The Telegraph*, November 03, 2015, http://www.telegraph. co.uk/news/uknews/11972509/Secret-wife-of-late-King-Fahd-of-Saudi-Arabia-wins-20million-in-damages-for-lavish-lifestyle.html

83 Fakkar Galal, "SAUDI ARABIA: Story behind the king's title," *Arab News*, January 27, 2015, retrieved November 2, 2017 from, http://www.arabnews.com/saudi-arabia/news/695351

84 Patrick Neil, *Saudi Arabian Foreign Policy: Conflict and Cooperation in Uncertain Times*, (I.B. Tauris, London, New York, 2016) (p.17)

85 Choksy Carol E. B., and Choksy Jamsheed K., "The Saudi Connection: Wahhabism and Global Jihad," *World Affairs Journal*, May/June 2015, http://www. worldaffairsjournal.org/article/saudi-connection-wahhabism-and-global-jihad.

86 Mackey Sandra, "Petro-Islam," World Heritage Encyclopedia, No Published Date, http://www.self.gutenberg.org/articles/eng/petro-islam

87 Lacey, Robert, *Inside the Kingdom: Kings, Clerics, Modernists, Terrorists, and the Struggle for Saudi Arabia*, (Viking, New York, 2009) p. 95

88 Johnson Toni, "The Organization of the Islamic Conference," *Council on Foreign Relations*, June 29, 2010, https://www.cfr.org/backgrounder/organization-islamic-conference

89 Patrick Neil, *Saudi Arabian Foreign Policy: Conflict and Cooperation in Uncertain Times*, (I.B. Tauris, London, New York, 2016) (Patrick, 2016).

90 Patrick Neil, *Saudi Arabian Foreign Policy: Conflict and Cooperation in Uncertain Times*, (I.B. Tauris, London, New York, 2016) (p. 19-20)

91 "What is Wahhabism? The reactionary branch of Islam from Saudi Arabia said to be 'the main source of global terrorism'," *The Telegraph News*, May 19, 2017, http://www.telegraph.co.uk/news/2016/03/29/what-is-wahhabism-the-reactionary-branch-of-islam-said-to-be-the/

92 Rasooldeen Mohammed., & Hassan Rashid, "Saudi Crown Prince pledges elimination of 'what is left of extremism' in near future," *Arab News*, October 25, 2017, http://www.arabnews.com/node/1182831/saudi-arabia

93 Raval Anjli, "US oil reserves surpass those of Saudi Arabia and Russia," Financial Times, July 4, 2016, https://www.ft.com/content/7525f1dc-41d6-11e6-9b66-0712b3873ae1

94 Partrick Neil, *Saudi Arabian Foreign Policy: Conflict and Cooperation in Uncertain Times*, (I.B. Tauris, London, New York, 2016) (p.47)

95 "Saudi Arabia clashes in eastern province of Qatif," *British Broadcast Corporation (BBC)*, October 4, 2017, http://www.bbc.com/news/world-middle-east-15169769

96 House Karen, Elliott, *On Saudi Arabia: Its People, Past, Religion, Fault Lines - and Future*, (Knopf, New York, 2012) (p.231)

97 By Martin Indyk Marin, "Amid the Arab Spring, Obama's dilemma over Saudi Arabia," *The Washington Post*, April 7, 2011, https://www.washingtonpost.

com/opinions/amid-the-arab-spring-obamas-dilemma-over-saudi-arabia/2011/04/07/AFhILDxC_story.html?utm_term=.4017a51936e2

98 Kalin Stephen, and Paul Katie, "Future Saudi king tightens grip on power with arrests including Prince Alwaleed," *Reuters*, November 5, 2017, https://www.reuters.com/article/us-saudi-arrests/future-saudi-king-tightens-grip-on-power-with-arrests-including-prince-alwaleed-idUSKBN1D506P

99 Bulos Nabih and, King Laura, "In gilded Saudi royal circles, corruption has long been a way of life," *Los Angeles Times*, November 8, 2017, http://www.latimes.com/world/middleeast/la-fg-saudi-corruption-20171108-story,amp.html

100 Bulos Nabih and, King Laura, "In gilded Saudi royal circles, corruption has long been a way of life," *Los Angeles Times*, November 8, 2017, http://www.latimes.com/world/middleeast/la-fg-saudi-corruption-20171108-story,amp.html

101 Stares Paul B., and Ighani Helia, "How Stable Is Saudi Arabia?" *Council on Foreign Relations*, May 15, 2017, https://www.cfr.org/expert-brief/how-stable-saudi-arabia

102 O'Sullivan C.D. (2012) FDR and Saudi Arabia: Forging a Special Relationship. In: FDR and the End of Empire. The World of the Roosevelts. Palgrave Macmillan, New York (O'Sullivan, 2012, p.90).

103 Lippman Thomas W., "The Day FDR Met Saudi Arabia's Ibn Saud," *The Link*, Volume 38, Issue 2, April-May 2005, http://www.ouramazingworld.org/uploads/4/3/8/6/43860587/vol38_issue2_2005.pdf (Lippman, 2005 p. 4).

104 Oualaalou David, *The Ambiguous Foreign Policy of the United States toward the Muslim World: More than a Handshake*, (Lanham, Maryland, Rowman and Littlefield, 2016) (Oualaalou, 2016, p. 77)

105 Brown Taylor K., "The secret US mission to heal Saudi King Ibn Saud," *British Broadcast Corporation (BBC)*, June 8, 2015, http://www.bbc.com/news/magazine-32965230

106 Brown Taylor K., "The secret US mission to heal Saudi King Ibn Saud," *British Broadcast Corporation (BBC)*, June 8, 2015, http://www.bbc.com/news/magazine-32965230

107 Doran Michael, "Obama is repeating Eisenhower's mistakes in the Middle East," *Los Angeles Times*, October 28, 2016, http://www.latimes.com/opinion/op-ed/la-oe-doran-obama-eisenhower-middle-east-mistake-20161028-story.html

108 Baalke, Caitlin, "A Political and Historic Analysis of the Relationship between the United States and Saudi Arabia: how the relationship between the United States and Saudi Arabia has influenced U.S. Foreign Policy in the Middle East" (2014). *Honors Projects*. 25. http://digitalcommons.spu.edu/honorsprojects/25 (Baalke, 2014, p. 15)

109 Perra Antonio, Kennedy and the Middle East: The Cold War, Israel and Saudi Arabia, (I.B.Tauris & Co.Ltd, London, New York, 2017)

110 Bronson Rachel, Thicker Than Oil: America's Uneasy Partnership with Saudi Arabia, (Oxford University Press, London, 2006) (Bronson, 2006, p.90)

111 Neff Donald, "Nixon Administration Ignores Saudi Warnings, Bringing On Oil Boycott," U.S. *Middle East Policy*, October/November 1997, pages 70-72, http://ifamericaknew.org/us_ints/oil-boycott.html

112 Mirzadegan Amin., "NIXON'S FOLLY THE WHITE HOUSE AND THE 1970S OIL PRICE CRISIS," The Yale Historical Review, 2016, https://historicalreview.yale.edu/sites/default/files/files/mirzadegan.pdf (p.44)

113 Marshall J., "Saudi Arabia and the Reagan Doctrine," Middle East Research and Information Project, n.d., http://www.merip.org/mer/mer155/saudi-arabia-reagan-doctrine

114 Niblock, Tim, *Saudi Arabia:Power, Legitimacy and Survival*) Routledge, Oxon, 2006. pp. 155-156) (Niblock, 2006).

115 Bayoumy Y., "Obama administration arms sales offers to Saudi top $115 billion," *Reuters*, September 7, 2016, https://www.reuters.com/article/us-usa-saudi-security/obama-administration-arms-sales-offers-to-saudi-top-115-billion-report-idUSKCN11D2JQ (Bayoumy, 2016)

116 "I think Islam Hates Us," *The New York Times*, Jan. 26, 2017, https://www.nytimes.com/2017/01/26/opinion/i-think-islam-hates-us.html

117 Lander M., Schmitt E., & Apuzo M., "$110 Billion Weapons Sale to Saudis Has Jared Kushner's Personal Touch," *The New York Times*, May 18, 2017, https://www.nytimes.com/2017/05/18/world/middleeast/jared-kushner-saudi-arabia-arms-deal-lockheed.html (Lander, 2017)

118 Oualaalou D., "The Dangerous Possibility of War with Iran," *HuffPost*, June 28, 2017, https://www.huffingtonpost.com/entry/the-dangerous-possibility-of-war-with-iran_us_5953ca34e4b0c85b96c65e49 (Oualaalou, 2017)

119 Meyer H and Carey G., "Even the Saudis Are Turning to Russia as Assad's Foes Lose Heart," *Bloomberg Politics*, September 7, 2017, https://www.bloomberg.com/news/articles/2017-09-08/even-the-saudis-are-turning-to-russia-as-assad-s-foes-lose-heart

120 Bronson R., "The United States and Saudi Arabia: Challenges Ahead," Middle East Institute, October 1, 2009, http://www.mei.edu/content/united-states-and-saudi-arabia-challenges-ahead (Branson, 2009. P. 84)

121 "U.S.-Saudi Relations," Council on Foreign Relations, May 12, 2017, https://www.cfr.org/backgrounder/us-saudi-relations

122 Aizhu C., "China's Iran oil imports to hit record on new production," Reuters, January 5, 2017, https://www.reuters.com/article/us-china-iran-oil/chinas-iran-oil-imports-to-hit-record-on-new-production-sources-idUSKBN14P15W

123 Altaqi A., and Essam A., "Chinese Ambitious Plans for Iran's Expanding Oil Exports," Orient Research Center, September 15, 2017, http://www.orientresearchcentre.com/en/oil-and-gas-issue-4-2-9-2017/

124 Wile R., "The US Is Sitting On A 200-Year Supply Of Oil," Business Insider, March 19, 2012, http://www.businessinsider.com/us-200-year-supply-oil-2012-3 (Wile, 2012)

125 By Collin Eaton Collin, "Permian Basin could yield 70 billion oil barrels in coming decades, IHS says," *Chron*, September 26, 2017, http://www.chron.com/business/energy/article/Permian-Basin-could-yield-70-billion-oil-barrels-12228760.php

126 Demongeot M., "Peak Oil Demand: China's Turn?" *Energy Intelligence*, April 2016, http://beta.energyintel.com/world-energy-opinion/peak-oil-demand-chinas-turn/

127 Branson Rachel, "Thicker Than Oil: America's Uneasy Partnership with Saudi Arabia," (Oxford University Press, New York, 2006, p. 251) (Holland, 2017)

128 Holland T., "A CRUDE PLAN: CHINESE OIL DEMAND COULD SEE SAUDI GIVE AMERICA THE SLIP," *South China Morning Post (SCMP)*, September 4, 2017, http://www.scmp.com/week-asia/opinion/article/2109397/crude-plan-chinese-oil-demand-could-see-saudi-give-america-slip

129 Fiedler M., "There is need for 'ecumenism' in Islam: The "Wars of Religion" in the 16th and 17th century might have ignited at a much earlier date," *Herald Malaysia*, January 5, 2016, http://www.heraldmalaysia.com/news/there-is-need-for-ecumenism-in-islam/27026/8

130 Nasr Vali, *"The Shia Revival: How conflicts within Islam will shape the future,"* (W. W. Norton & Company, New York and London, 2016). (Nasr, 2016, p. 40)

131 Oualaalou David, *"Volatile State: Iran in the Nuclear Age,"* (Indian University Press, Bloomington, Indiana, 2018). (Oualaalou, 2018, p. 192)

132 In 2016, I wrote, "To highlight the level of corruption the Palestinian liberation Organization leadership have engaged in, an estimated $11.5million from that financial assistance was diverted from Switzerland to two bank accounts in Paris, France. The bank accounts were under Mrs. Arafat's name." David Oualaalou, *The Ambiguous Foreign Policy of the United States toward the Muslim World: More than a Handshake* (Lanham, Maryland: Lexington Books (Imprint of the Rowman and Littlefield Publishing Group, 2016), 49.

133 Finn T., "Row over haj pilgrimage helps fuel Qatar rift," *Reuters*, August 22, 2017, https://ca.reuters.com/article/topNews/idCAKCN1B21IR-OCATP

134 Alsubaie S., "Politicization of Hajj over the years," *Al-Arabiya*, August 30, 017, http://english.alarabiya.net/en/views/news/middle-east/2017/08/30/Politics-of-Hajj-over-the-years.html

135 As argued in my previous writing: "Iran's latest deal with Total is only the beginning: "I can assure you this isn't the last one. We'll see other contracts being made within the next few weeks," Deputy Minister of Petroleum for International Affairs Amir Hossein Zamaninia said on the sidelines of a conference in Istanbul this past Tuesday. Mr. Zamaninia was referring to Austria, Norway, Sweden,

the United Kingdom, Germany, and Denmark, who expressed interest in investment opportunities in Iran. Denmark, for instance, proposed a $1 billion investment contribution to Iran's development plans. Iran itself already stands to reap about 65% to 70% of the international investments so far, estimated at $200 billion. Thus, Saudi Arabia's strategy of choking Iran's economy through oil prices is a failed one." Oualaalou D., "Saudis Losing Oil War as Iran Gains Power," *HuffPost*, July 14, 2017, https://www.huffingtonpost.com/entry/saudis-losing-oil-war-as-iran-gains-power_us_59690af5e4b022bb9372b15a

136 Nakhoul S., Bassam L., and Perry T., "How Saudi Arabia turned on Lebanon's Hariri," *Reuters*, November 11, 2017, https://www.reuters.com/article/us-lebanon-politics-hariri-exclusive/exclusive-how-saudi-arabia-turned-on-lebanons-hariri-idUSKBN1DB0QL

137 Guarnieri G., "Saudi Arabia's Crown Prince Bought the World's Most Expensive Mansion for $300 Million, and a $500 Million Yacht," *Newsweek*, December 18, 2017, https://www.yahoo.com/news/saudi-arabia-crown-prince-bought-185126588.html

138 "Saudi general 'may have been tortured to death' during Ritz-Carlton crackdown," The Telegraph, March 12, 2018, https://www.yahoo.com/news/saudi-general-apos-may-tortured-140851563.html

139 Ighani H., "Managing the Saudi-Iran Rivalry," *Council on Foreign Relations*, October 25, 2016, https://www.cfr.org/sites/default/files/pdf/2016/10/Workshop_Report_CPA_Saudi_Iran_Rivalry_OR.pdf (Ighani 2016)

140 Henderson, S., "How the War in Yemen Explains the Future of Saudi Arabia," *The Atlantic*, November 8, 2017, https://www.theatlantic.com/international/archive/2017/11/saudi-arabia-iran-yemen-houthi-salman/545336/

141 Oualaalou David, ███████████████████████ As argued in my previous writing, "Based on how much money Saudi Arabia provides Pakistan, one infers that, if and when the kingdom needs something in return, like a nuclear bomb, Pakistan would reciprocate." *Volatile State: Iran in the Nuclear Age* (Indiana University Press, Bloomington, Indiana, 2018), 124.

142 Hassan Syed, R., Johnson K., and Macfie N., "Pakistan to send troops to Saudi Arabia to train and advise," *Reuters*, February 16, 2018, https://www.reuters.com/article/us-pakistan-saudi/pakistan-to-send-troops-to-saudi-arabia-to-train-and-advise-idUSKCN1G00YI

143 Harrison Ross., "Saudi Arabia is weakening itself and strengthening Iran," *Foreign Policy*, July 6, 2017, http://foreignpolicy.com/2017/07/06/saudi-arabia-is-weakening-itself-and-strengthening-iran/

144 Oualaalou David, "Falling Oil Prices and Geopolitics," *The HuffPost*, January 20, 2015, https://www.huffingtonpost.com/entry/falling-oil-prices-and-ge_b_6498002.html

145 Rigg B., "The Decline And Fall Of The House Of Saud?" *Eurasia Review*, April 22, 2016, http://www.eurasiareview.com/22042016-the-decline-and-fall-of-the-house-of-saud-oped/

146 Gordon P., Yadlin A., and Heistein A., "The Qatar Crisis: Causes, Implications, Risks, and the Need for Compromise," *The Institute for National Security Studies*, June 13, 2017, http://www.inss.org.il/publication/qatar-crisis-causes-implications-risks-need-compromise/

147 Harrison Ross., "Saudi Arabia is weakening itself and strengthening Iran," *Foreign Policy*, July 6, 2017, http://foreignpolicy.com/2017/07/06/saudi-arabia-is-weakening-itself-and-strengthening-iran/

148 Dabashi H., "Muhammad bin Kushner, Jared bin Salman, Daffy Duck & Co," *Aljazeera*, December 3, 2017, http://www.aljazeera.com/indepth/opinion/muhammad-bin-kushner-jared-bin-salman-daffy-duck-171203092338779.html

149 Khashoggi J., "Saudi Arabia wasn't always this repressive. Now it's unbearable," *The Washington Post*, September 18, 2017, https://www.washingtonpost.com/amphtml/news/global-opinions/wp/2017/09/18/saudi-arabia-wasnt-always-this-repressive-now-its-unbearable/

150 Sherwell P., Mendick R., and Meo N., "Egypt: Hosni Mubarak used last 18 days in power to secure his fortune," *The Telegraph*, February 12, 2011, http://www.telegraph.co.uk/news/worldnews/africaandindianocean/egypt/8320912/Egypt-Hosni-Mubarak-used-last-18-days-in-power-to-secure-his-fortune.html

151 Domm P., "US oil production tops 10 million barrels a day for first time since 1970," Market Insider, CNBC, January 31, 2018, https://www.cnbc.com/2018/01/31/us-oil-production-tops-10-million-barrels-a-day-for-first-time-since-1970.html

152 I argue, "One thing is sure: The region's geopolitics play to Iran's favor. The KSA needs to accept that it can't influence oil prices to return to their pre-2014 level of $120/barrel. That's a bygone era!" Oualaalou D, "Saudis Losing Oil War as Iran Gains Power" *The Huffighton Post*, July 14, 2017, https://www.huffingtonpost.com/entry/saudis-losing-oil-war-as-iran-gains-power_us_59690af5e4b022bb9372b15a

153 "Lebanese TV host charged with defaming Saudi crown prince," Associated Press, January 26, 2018, http://www.chicagotribune.com/news/nationworld/sns-bc-ml--lebanon-20180126-story.html

154 "Saudi Arabia: Prominent Clerics Arrested," *Human Rights Watch*, September 15, 2017, https://www.hrw.org/news/2017/09/15/saudi-arabia-prominent-clerics-arrested

155 "UK lawyers: Remove Saudi from UN Human Rights Council," Aljazeera, January 31, 2018, http://www.aljazeera.com/news/2018/01/uk-lawyers-remove-saudi-human-rights-council-180131114753148.html

156 Smith L., "Yemen: More than 50,000 children expected to die of starvation and disease by end of year," Independent, November 15, 2017, http://www.

independent.co.uk/news/world/middle-east/yemen-war-saudi-arabia-children-deaths-famine-disease-latest-figures-a8057441.html

157 I have argued elsewhere, "It is a challenging proposition to explain to outsiders how Muslims can be "the best people evolved for human kind" according to the Quran; yet leaders in Muslim and Arab countries figure among the worst humanity could imagine in our present age of anxiety." Oualaalou D., "Islamic leaders must condemn widespread hypocrisy," *The Waco Tribune-Herald*, August 10, 2014, http://www.wacotrib.com/opinion/columns/board_of_contributors/david-oualaalou-board-of-contributors-islamic-leaders-must-condemn-widespread/article_d41ac38b-39a3-568f-95b7-f2f5c3bc018e.html

Index

Pahlavi, Mohammed Reza, 84, 114, 118
Pakistan, xviii, 19, 23–24, 26, 50–51,
    54, 56, 70, 109, 114, 118,
    120–21
Palestine, 39, 108
Paris, France, 108
Partrick, Neil, 66–67, 71, 75
Paul, Katie, 79
Pentagon, Washington D.C., United
    States of America, xviii, 5,
    24–25, 93
Permian Basin, Texas, United States,
    74, 101
Perra, Antonio, 87
Persia, 32, 55
Persian Gulf, the, 4, 36–38, 49, 51, 75,
    99, 126, 129
Philippines, 19, 24, 50, 65
Phippen, Weston, 18
Pollack, Kenneth, 56
Powell, Colin, 94

Q

Qahtani, Ali al-, 115
Qandahar, Afghanistan, 26
Qatar,
    Arabic in, 39
    China and, 114
    indigenous resources in, 75, 102
    Iran and, 113
    Saudi Arabian conflict with, xv, 2,
        5–7, 36, 55, 109, 119
    Saudi Arabian blockade on, 61, 116
Qatif, Saudi Arabia, 3, 37, 43, 76

R

Rasheed, Madawi al-, 33
Rashid, al-, 34
Rasooldeen, Mohammed, 73
Raval, Anjli, 74
Rawalpindi, Pakistan, 26

Reagan, Ronald, 90–91, 97
Riegg, Ryan, 46, 48
Ritz-Carlton, Riyadh, Saudi Arabia,
    The, xi, 78, 131, 137
Riyadh, Saudi Arabia,
    Abdul Wahhab in, 33
    capital moved to, 34, 37, 48
    cultural norms in, 54
    geopolitical rivalry in, 114–20
    ideological rivalry with Iran in,
        118–20
    oil in, 70, 101, 113
    Russia and, 15–17
    Saad Hariri and, 112
    Saudi Arabia and, 3
    Tehran and, xvii, 1, 9, 12–13
    Terrorism and, 72
    Trump and, 96–98, 103
    United States and, 16–17, 20, 25,
        46, 53, 78, 85
    Wahhabism and, 24, 43
    Yemen and, 67
Roosevelt, Franklin D., 82–83
Rumsfeld, Donald H., 94
Russia,
    influence in Middle East, xix, 19,
        57, 104, 115–17, 129
    Iran and, 3–9, 12, 96, 114
    Libya and, 2
    OPEC and, xiv–xv, 6, 102, 113
    Saudi Arabia and, 1, 7, 13–15, 56,
        98
    United States and, 58, 74, 95–96
    weapon sales of, 45–46, 96

S

Saadani, Hala, 17
Saipov, Sayfullo, 99
Saleh, Ali Abdullah, 119
Sanaa, Yemen, 17

oil wealth of, xiii, 29, 35, 39,
74–78
oppression in, 127, 132–33
population of, 38, 79
role in Middle East, xiv, xviii–xx,
2–3, 7, 12, 15, 27, 33, 35–
36, 47, 50, 57, 59, 61, 95,
98, 105, 112, 114, 119, 121,
126, 130, 135, 137
Russia, relationship with, xv, 1, 7,
13–15, 56, 91, 98, 116,
Shi'a minority, treatment of, 3
succession issues in, 21, 44, 81, 136
support and tolerance of by United
States, xv, 7, 48, 58, 84–85,
90–91, 94, 96, 105
United States and, xv–xvi, xix,
27, 56, 78, 82–83, 86–89,
92–93, 97–105, 140
Turkey and, 119
use of Iraq to mend relations with
Iran, 1, 4, 7, 9, 12
Wahhabist elements of, xviii, 19,
35, 50–53, 62–66, 68–69,
72–73, 118
Yemen and, 4–7, 13–15, 37, 60–
61, 71
Sayyaf, Abu, 19, 65
Schramm, Madison, 9
Semawi, Muhammad Ne'ma Al-, 26
Seville, Spain, 31
Sheikh, Abdulaziz Ibn Abdullah
Abdullatif Al Ash-, 23
Sheikh, Mohammed bin Ibrahim
Al-, 73
Sin Ibn Ali, 32
Singapore, 102
Sisi, Abdel Fattah el-, 119
Somalia, 19, 22–24, 26, 65
Soviet Union, 87

invasion of Afghanistan by, 13–
14, 25
Saudi Arabia and, 91, 116
United States and, 84, 120
Spain, 31–32
Stalin, Joseph, 84
Sudan, 24, 39, 50–51, 54, 56, 70
Sweden, 9
Syria,
Arabic in, 39–40
civil war in, xii, 2–3, 22, 14–16,
59, 98
extremism in, 22
geopolitical shifts in, xiv
Iran and, 119
proxy wars in, 114
Qatar and, 109
Russia and, xix, 13, 15
Saladin and, 66–67
security challenges in, 61
Six Day War of 1967 and, 88
Sunni rebels in, xv, 5
United States and, 48

T

Tabatabai, Ariane M., 9
Taif, Saudi Arabia, 37
Tartus, Syria, xix
Tehran, Iran
Riyadh and, xvii, 1, 9, 12, 114,
116–18
Saudi Arabia and, 5
Shi'a and, 110
US Embassy in, 90
Texas, United States of America, xii,
74, 101
Truman, Harry S., 17, 84–85
Trump, Donald J.,
dangerous rhetoric and, 6, 8–9, 96
Iran sanctions and, xv–xvi, 9, 56,
58

Made in the USA
Middletown, DE
16 November 2018